Bare Fields: The Russians in Gallipoli, 1920–21

Ivan Lukash

Bare Fields

The Russians in Gallipoli, 1920–21

Translated by Elevenfortyseven

ANTELOPE HILL PUBLISHING

Maybe we are dead men, if Russia herself is dead.
Maybe we are not needed if Russia is not needed.
But she is alive, and don't you realize
that we, like her, are alive too?

– Lieutenant Misha

Contents

ELEVENFORTYSEVEN

Few conflicts have been as acute as the Russian Civil War of 1917. As many as ten million lives were lost; most of these are contained within Russia herself, and most of these are the lives of entirely innocent civilians. And what does this conflict have to show for itself? An exodus of Russia's greatest patriots, who never gave up and formed an intellectual powerhouse in the White emigre movement, publishing powerful literary attacks in Berlin, Paris, and Sofia (most notably Ivan Ilyin); the unraveling of the Second World War (an abundance of evidence indicates that Stalin was preparing, through all possible means, to invade Europe and suffocate her within the decadent grip of the Marxist Internationale); a failed state, its eventual collapse, and the suffering of millions among its ruins; and a country whose people were left to yearn for some semblance of historical stability.

To set the scene: two sides, two warring ideologies—the monarchist Whites and the communist Reds; the fields, cities, and rivers of Russia as their battlefield. Tsar Nicholas II and his family had been taken hostage, to be executed in cold blood only sixteen months later (thankfully, today's majority of Russian and international public recognizes this act for what it truly was: a criminal slaughter). Red soldiers, men who had previously sworn an oath to protect their country and its citizens, are pillaging the streets, murdering landowners and shopkeepers, stealing, and raping their countrymen's women "in the name of the Revolution." Yet, despite all this chaotic pain, despite this ruptured boil spreading its rot all over the country's healthy, fertile body, the people do not resist. There is a well-known anecdote conveyed to us by a certain man of military talent: he tells of his return to St. Petersburg following some travels and finds himself shocked by the utter depravity and destruction sweeping through the country's former capital. As he walks through the streets and observes all this, he stumbles across a theater, one he used to frequent, and decides to peek inside in order to gauge the extent of the damages, or determine whether the Red pillagers had made it that far yet. He walks in, and, to his surprise, sees that the theater is packed with men and women watching a performance, laughing, clapping. The man stood petrified, wondering how this could be: their city is under murderous demolition, and yet the citizens enjoy a show, peacefully, unknowingly—carelessly....

The esteemed man above was Baron Pyotr Wrangel. Eventually, he would lead the entire White Army and oversee the historic evacuation of the Crimea—an event that saved over 145,000 lives—when it became clear that the existing fronts of the White Army would no longer hold against the spreading Red terror in 1920. Aboard 126 ships, Wrangel's fleet, also known as the Russian Squadron, sailed to Constantinople, where other White emigres (intellectuals, artists, academics, veterans of the Imperial Army caught abroad at the time of the struggle) had been patiently waiting for the Bolshevik atrocities to end. Most of the civilians settled there, with their families and many of the soldiers, but a thirty-thousand strong section of the Russian Squadron decided to settle in Greece's Gallipoli (Gelibolu today; *Kallipolis* in the Greek meaning "Beautiful City"). For the next three years, the patriots of the White Army would live in limbo, in temporarily frozen history: the sun rises, the sun falls, the soldiers pray, have tea, exercise, and swim in the glistening sea. A profound feeling of loss, of irritability due to inaction, permeates every living corner of their massive camp. Some men await a return to their homeland, others revel in the nightly activities and overdrink, and a few are driven to an impatient suicide....

The author of this book, this living description, Ivan Sozontovich Lukash (1892–1940), is among the men of Gallipoli. Born to a veteran of the Russo-Turkish War, Lukash is most famous for his "interviews" of Anton Turkul and Vladimir Manstein (see pages 47–56)—two legendary men of Mikhail Gordeyevich Drozdovsky's Regiment, a famed unit of men who completed a daring campaign from Romania's Jassy to the Don in only two months, averaging forty to forty-five miles walked a day, recruiting over two thousand men on their way to the Volunteer cause—which serve as a morbid, yet glaring highlight in *Bare Fields*. His purpose is clear: to document the life and emotions of the camps, in order to preserve the memory of Russia's displaced patriots. Lukash sees a collective of ambitious young men left with nothing—no home, no *patria*, no money, and, in some cases, no health. Yet, his lines consistently reverberate with a certain kind of strength: the swarming psychological despair is offset by a sturdy carelessness toward the severe physical, and thus mental, condition. The patriots live for the White struggle; they live by the memory of their homeland, and by a certainty in its salvation. His imagery is persistently dry, gray, ageing and aged, bronze. Gallipoli is a cemetery, its only colors the brilliant uniforms and outfits of the Whites, their different colors determined by their belonging to X or Y regiment. The men are bronzed by the sun, lashed by it; their uniforms are red, white, blue, with accents of yellows on their banners, black eagles, and, at times, dark-green gangrene and rot, and crimson blood, all set to the shimmering waves of the bright, blue, never-ceasing sea.

This piece serves no ulterior purposes; it was not penned in order to propagandize, nor is it in any form a call to action. Lukash presents to us a Russian mosaic, each tile set perfectly to the next. This mosaic, enriched by the most heartfelt yearning, would only make its return to Russia following the collapse of the Communist regime. At times, the author humors us with an anecdote or an amusing accident, and at other times, he laments over a young woman and his memories of her as a schoolgirl amidst the winters of St. Petersburg. She is older now, but still so fair; she spends her days watching the soldiers tire at their daily work from the heights of a terribly dilapidated house, through a window terribly broken, terribly frozen.... She, and the other loving wives present, are forced to endure this pain in a soldierly way; Russia forces them to endure this; their *love* for her presents no other option. A man once said, when asked about the role of a Russian wife, "When her husband shoots at his enemies, she will be there to supply the ammo."

Lukash covers one single year in the three-year timeline of the Gallipoli camps. A frozen winter, a blazing summer, rainy fall and spring: the soldiers wait on and on, through it all, patiently. They wait for their Motherland to beckon; some do not know if she ever will, while others have never been more certain of her eventual summons.

Sometime around 1921, Lukash would leave for Sofia, Bulgaria, where this book would be published a year later. From Sofia, Lukash would move to Berlin and form a close association with Vladimir Nabokov, the then twenty-four-year-old future author of the infamous *Lolita*. Of their association it was said, "Never again would Nabokov have such close contact in his work with any writer as he did with the cocky Lukash." Indeed, they would spend the next three years co-writing plays and ballets to accompany various pieces by composers. This was the only instance of Nabokov ever agreeing to work with another writer, and, perhaps, after reading this book, the reason for this will become that much clearer to the dear reader.

Lukash eventually moved to France, where he penned several historical novels and worked as a co-editor for a Russian emigre newspaper, *Revival*, until his death from tuberculosis in 1940. It is of note to mention that Ivan Ilyin also penned articles for this newspaper, as the ideological head of the White movement; it is unknown whether they ever met or became acquainted through letters, but their articles read that much better when taken together, with the knowledge of the events that fill in the blank spaces of Russia's twentieth-century mosaic history.

No introductions can do justice to the sentiment, the *feeling*, presented in this work. It is an exhortation of the true Russian spirit: gentle, clearheaded, unyielding, melancholy yet optimistic. Few peoples can understand the adversities faced by the Russian nation throughout history, and the importance of this *first* fight against Communism cannot be understated. The White Army lives on in every patriot, in every man who is aware of the significance of their task, of the significance of history itself, with the White Army as a prototype of future struggle and *Bare Fields* a meditation on its daily, at times uneventful, but deeply significant life.

When the coals die out, touch them with your tongs, strike the charred black embers, and the sparks will rush and dance—sit closer, lean into the heat, and listen to the whispers of the fire.

You see: the walls are crumbling silently and the crimson towers fall, lightly whistling. You see how, glistened by their scarlet armor, the knights arose, and then the flaming monks rushed away, swirling. You see the hurling of burning banners.

Sit closer, bend forward, so that the crimson light illuminates your face, and listen to the whispers of the fire.

Listen....

General Alexander Kutepov (1882–1930)

Kutep–Pasha

Her collarbones are showing through the white cambric of her blouse. Her collarbones, like two soft wings, spread across her chest. We're sitting on the floor, on a striped mattress. When she turns her head, I can see how her golden, auburn locks curl over the white nape of her neck. They curl in the same way they did long ago in St. Petersburg, when she was a little girl, when she wore a brown dress with a white lace apron and went to the gymnasium. She had a small, green, Morocco-leather briefcase with a silver lock and key.

We're sitting on the floor. But, where we sit is not a room, but the top landing of a wooden staircase. The wooden steps have caved in, and we have to be very careful to lift our feet so as to not fall into the black pits. The decrepit banisters shake beneath my hand.

The landing is where she lives. The walls are smeared with gray lime and covered with cracks and greenish lichens. I prop my head against a pasted scrap of yellowed newspaper. Above me are printed black letters: "End to the Bolsheviks." And when the burned-out scraps are pressed, they crackle under the back of my head. Bedbug holes are glued over by the scraps; the lime is covered in brown smears of blood. This gray, half-ruined Greek house is a real bedbug den.

And there is no window on the landing. No window—it was knocked out, and the cavity in the wall is semi-curtained by a blanket. The yellow blanket hung there during the winter too, when wet snow swept over the landing and we had to shake off white mounds of frost from our pillows.

There is now a sullen heat. The air crushes, like an incandescent millstone, and from the brown plaza, where the cargo trucks are parked, a prickly, gray dust blows onto the landing. . . .

She has been living here for almost a year now, she and her husband, a pilot officer with blue, slightly faded eyes.

"Listen, the first parade was outside our window: in the fall, in the rain. Their green overcoats were steaming. I listened to how they trampled outside the window. They had rags wrapped around their feet instead of boots; their boots were split open and all their toes were out. They stood ankle-deep in mud, in the rain. They were ordered to line up, but they didn't know how to line up. They'd forgotten everything. They crowded and trampled. . . . They were so sweet, so dear, you know? I cried."

I look into her familial, brown eyes, and I recall, softly and quietly, the brown dress of a gymnasium student and a silver key to a green briefcase. I recollect how, during the winter, she would come in from the cold with her midshipman, and her cheeks would be burning, and her brown hair would smell of a frosty smoke, and beads of St. Petersburg frost would be melting on her silky, brown, fox-fur coat. . . .

"And you see what kind of dandies we have here now, all in white shirts and all in boots. They print their footsteps into the ground. But when they sing, I always cry. I can't hear the words, but I know that they're about Russia, and I feel such a longing— you understand."

The autumn parade took place the day, perhaps, when General Kutepov rode on horseback into the campsite for the first time. The rain was pelting down, and the wet, dark tatters of clouds dragged down, clinging smokily to the mountains. The horse was up to its belly in the clay tangles of the road.

Parade of the 1st Army Corps in the Gallipoli camps

They allocated a spot for the Russian camp on the land of some Turkish colonel, in the valley, near the mountains, where an English camp had been during the Great War. The English called their camp "The Valley of Roses and Death," because of the sprawling thickets of scarlet rosehips creeping along the ravines above the valley's river, and because many English riflemen died of snake bites and mosquito fever.

The valley billowed with gray smoke. Kutepov looked around and struck his horse hard in its side with his spurs, and turned back to Gallipoli.

There, by the breakwater, where the tide rumbled like cannon fire, stood the troops who had landed on the shore at nightfall. Having spread their overcoats on the mud, men with typhoid lay there. The soldiers were tired and slept, having covered themselves, and their heads, with wet overcoats. There, the Junkers, stomping their chilling feet, were singing. They sang because they were cold, because they wanted to howl from hunger, and it was getting difficult to clench their red and wet, cold-stricken fingers. The wind and rain sounded a vague howl.

"*Mama, Mama,* what will we do when the winter colds come...."

This song about their mothers was the first Russian song that the autumn Gallipoli had heard.

"When I turned my horse around and rode back, that's when I understood what I had to do," the general told his relatives about the first days of Gallipoli.

On the breakwater, where the tide rushed in herds of white wolves, women, children, and soldiers were huddled together in the cold rain, soaked to the skin. This was an exhausted crowd, hungry, beggars, dumped out of the black innards of the transportation vehicles, human dust stirred up by the wind, moaning in the icy rain....

Ripped epaulettes, damp overcoats like sacks over their heads. No one knew which unit, which regiment was on the breakwater. On the breakwater everything was muddled together.

And under the rain the rolled-up banners were soaking, steaming, and withering.

Kutepov entered the crowd. Somebody didn't salute him. Kutepov shouted sharply, "Salute! Are you a refugee or a soldier?"

Kutepov understood that without discipline there would be no army, and that there was nothing small or unimportant in discipline, and that in discipline everything is important and everything is most essential—even a hand not raised to the forehead and an epaulet sewn on improperly. Kutepov knew over what trifles, over what petty details the great disintegration of the greatest army had begun....

And so during the very first days, Kutepov ordered someone to be arrested and put in the guardhouse. He, probably, thought this way: Russia is waiting for the army, and in order to preserve the army, discipline must be preserved. He, probably, thought that this was what Russia needed.

And from here, from the breakwater, where everything was muddled together and the banners had drooped, came the story of the famous Gallipoli guardhouse, or "the Guba" in common parlance....

Kutepov was a determined, ironclad general. When he was still a gymnasium-boy, he cultivated his will to a special degree: he forced himself to wake up at night, put on his uniform, and march, parade, struggling against sleep. He is a kind and simple man, he has a squinted, affectionate grin, his laughter is contagious, and his broad, tanned merchant's face resembles the stout face of a Muscovite steward.

Kutepov is a man of simple tastes and simple sensibilities. He is all wide, low, and squat. And when he stands, he burrows into the ground. All his strength is in his legs, and he looks entirely like that bronze Bitiug, burrowed into the swampy St. Petersburg causeway, who guards St. Petersburg with the bearded, downcast tsar.[1]

The story of the Guba has begun. The Guba is the strong arm of

---

[1] Referring to the mounted monument of Alexander III.

army life; the Guba is the core tone of the military shoulder straps and the military everyday life.

At the square little bay of Gallipoli, crowded with light fleet boats, which sway their gray masts and themselves are like mincing birds on the dock, where small flocks of straw chairs from Turkish cafes are nestled on the gray cobblestones, stand mustached Russian sentries in faded shirts, with rifles over their shoulders. Behind the wooden bridges the wide wall of the Guba rises, lined with gray slabs.

They say that the gray wall was built by Venetian knights. They say that in the bare stone casemate, under the black, soot-covered beams of the ceiling, they found Zaporozhian inscriptions, prayers to Jesus from the captive men of Ostapy.

All of Gallipoli is like a dusty, sun-scorched highway of history. This is where Xerxes thrashed the Hellespont with rusty chains. Near Gallipoli stood the tents of the Crusaders. On the other side of the bay stretches a yellow ribbon of houses in the Greek town where Aristophanes was born.

Gallipoli, the City of Beauty, has now become a deserted Bare Field, as the Russian soldiers nicknamed it. Centuries have dusted away, and now a dusty cemetery is scattered here. Everywhere, along the narrow streets, above the white plazas, by the sea, white turbans, cut from marble, rise to the sun on the crooked pillars of Turkish graves.

By the gray walls, destroyed by an earthquake and the firing of English ships, and over the sandy slopes, brown burdock sways, rustling dryly. Slender lizards wiggle, slithering along the tombstones, where centuries-old dust lodges in the serpentine curls of Arabic letters. Burnt grass rustles under one's footsteps. The whitish sand burns the soles of the feet. And everywhere the dry rustle of burdock and lizards. . . .

And beyond Gallipoli, up to the blue, ghostly mountains: golden wheat fields, where black flocks of jackdaws fly in black flakes. The air trembles with the anxious flutter of their wings. The gray stone mills, like castle towers, barely move their round sailcloth wings, bound at the edges with thick rope, just like black spiderwebs. Knotty and austere plane trees, strewn with gray ashes of dust, rustle by the roadside. Under them, at midday, enormous blue-gray oxen with outspread white horns rest. The oxen's kind, dark, and moist pupils bulge out, and their wrinkled nostrils ooze, while on their soft, gray scruffs, blue, glassy evil eye beads glisten in the sun.

If you look around, you will see a golden mirage, golden heavy dust, white turbans incandescent with the sun, and the blue sea behind them.

The sea is blue, with white trembling trails of foam, humming with the steady breath of the unceasing tide. The breath of the sea rushes over Gallipoli. It departs, it returns, drenches the gray sand with its salty dew, and rumbles with a resounding rumble, as if down below, by the dark rocks, sloping like a turtle's back, where, whistling, noisy foam pours, herds of heavy-sighing horses are galloping, clattering their hoofs.

Over the blue sea, mountains hang like blue ghosts. So tender, so blue, and so feminine. . . .

The City of Beauty, Gallipoli—where the white feathers of knights' helmets glistened in the sun, where slave girls from all over the East were traded, over by the gleaming aqueducts—has been burned out for centuries and has now fallen asleep as a scorched, dusty cemetery.

And only at the Guba, in the harbor, life stirs.

On straw chairs, with their legs spread and their bellies out, wrapped in dirty, red sashes, the Turks sit. Shoeshiners and grimy little Spanish Jews sit by the water, loudly drumming their brushes on their black boxes.

"Shine, shine ... *Russ*, very good. . . ."

Under the canvas awnings of the stalls, where it smells of cinnamon and onions, green-yellow heads of melons are stacked on burlap, tomatoes show their crimson, plump cheeks, and matte bunches of grapes hang from dark, wet baskets.

White fleet boats, with blue and green patterns on the sides, with soft breasts like swans, that sail to Athens, and to Odessa, sway their slender masts in the sky. In the sunny water, the shadows of the masts, the green and blue stripes, and the white sails intertwine and ripple. . . .

Some black Senegalese tramped along, their glossy backs glistening with oil, in dove-colored helmets. The Russian soldiers call them "Earrings." A Greek, shaking the gold charms of a chain, hurries somewhere, shifting his yellow canotier to the back of his head, and sweat hangs like a drop from his hunchbacked, predatory nose. Some short-legged Frenchmen, sweaty and red as if from a hot bath, passed by, chatting merrily. A platoon of white Russian Junkers print their footsteps into the ground, swinging their arms in unison.

The city fountain is by the harbor. The broad, dark slabs of sidewalk are always wet and shiny. The water rings fresh and glistens. Buckets and tin cans jingle joyfully. . . .

It's cool in the cafe by the harbor. Sunny, watery streaks form from the water along the dry ceiling. The white lime of the walls has fresh murals: hookahs with crimson tubes in golden weave; bottles filled with clear, golden wine; silver-red parrots; and huge, white Russian daisies—painted by a Russian. Russian murals are in all Turkish cafes by the harbor.

The harbor of Gallipoli

In the evening, in the Olympium coffee house by the breakwater, they light four copper kerosene lamps with reflectors. And there, in the evening, a Russian officer's wife plays the old romances "Para gnedykh" and "Ah da pust' svet osuzhdaet" on the piano....[2]

And on the rickety veranda, which overlooks the sea, on a floating plateau, between the peeling, narrow, white-painted tables, walks a Russian restaurant girl. Her moist eyes are lined and her lips are touched with carmine, like all Russian restaurant girls in Turkey.

But she will not be bothered here. She won't be harmed by strangers here. Her arms will not be pinched to the point of bruising, as they do in the cafes of Istanbul. She is one of their own,

---

[2] "A Pair of Bays" and "Oh Yes, Let the World Judge."

the Regimental Masha, traveling with the regiment all the way back from Rostov and Novorossiysk....

In the fall there had been thefts, and there had been robberies, and in the evenings, under the lights of the cafes, pale Russian soldiers came out of the darkness for alms. And there once was such a story: to a Greek tavern, where some boatmen who had been drinking were wailing catlike songs, came a soldier, and the boatmen played a joke; they poured a glass of vodka and stacked a handful of copper lepta. "Here, Russian, take the drink and the money, but get down on your knees first."

That soldier came in from the fall rain. During those days, lousy, ragged, and hungry Russian tramps, who had been thrown ashore from their ships, would crawl into warm cafes, to the fire, and take one cup of thick, bitter coffee to share between ten of them, if only to get some heat, if only to warm up. During those days, the sea rumbled and the cold rain pelted into the ground those who were sleeping. During those days, a cold, black night lingered upon everyone's souls.

The Russian pauper stumbled about, left stains with his footpads, and suddenly began to kneel. And that's when the officer's wife, a real restaurant girl, gasped, threw up her hands, swept the shot glasses and the stack of tinkling lepta off the table, and rushed to the soldier.

"Don't you dare. Don't get down on your knees—you're a Russian."

And there was, probably, something frightening in her cry, because the pauper ran away, and the black-mustached, hairy, tenacious, ape-like boatmen got up silently and left.

This officer's wife's name is Vika. She has cropped blonde hair, an ashy mole on her round chin, and bright and cheerful dimples when she smiles. Last year she graduated from a gymnasium in Simferopol. Her Kolya fell ill with tuberculosis, and now she has to work.

"Well, somehow, somehow...somehow everyone endures," she said, and blushed instantly, fingering the clinking glasses with her thin, tanned fingers.

This happened in December, when the cold night lingered upon everyone's souls, when people dreamed of overturned limbers, of blown-up armored cars, of blood and rain and the boiler rooms of ships, where indelible black dust climbed into every furrow of the skin.

This happened in December.... And now there are no Russian paupers in Gallipoli. Now the tenacious Greeks bow respectfully and the Turks slowly greet the Russians, putting two fingers to their fezzes.

Sleepy hairdressers in sun-drenched stalls, peering at your face in the dull, fly-infested mirror, will carefully and kindly hold the tip of your nose with two fingers, smelling of onions and tobacco, and ask, like real Russian hairdressers, "Haircut, shave? Very good."

The black Senegalese-Earrings do not understand the Greeks, and the Greeks do not understand the Earrings. And they talk to each other in Russian. The Earrings bare their teeth, swivel the whites of their eyes silently and terribly, and babble hotly in Russian, "How much does it cost? Give me more.... Come here.... No good."

The Turkish women write down long and flowing Russian phrases that they hear from the officer-tenants. They write them down in gentle scribbled ribbons and recite them, clapping their hands and laughing joyfully, listening to the incomprehensible music of a foreign language.

Turkish women, flexible as cats, fall in love instantly and suddenly with the fair-haired giaours, and up to ten Anfehs and Fatimas have already become the wives of Russian officers.

Russian is the spoken language of Gallipoli. Little Turkish girls, brown, quick-eyed, resembling little fleas, shuffling barefoot in the dust and hoisting their satin salwars in their arms, sing, squealing terribly, songs from Odessa—sometimes "Akh zachem eta noch,'" sometimes "Polyubil vsey dushoy yia devitsu."[3]

Greek boys, all long-nosed and all with inflated round bellies, play-pretend as soldiers, from the morning, and speak commands in Russian: "Attention.... Foooorwaaaard march...."

There are no more Russian tramps or Russian paupers in Gallipoli. There is now an impoverished Russian gentleman, cleanly dressed, big, strong, kind, but very impoverished, to the point that sometimes we have to procure for him a wedding ring, a pair of boots, a deck of cards, an American shirt, and a shabby fur, brought all the way from Moscow. It was not without Kutepov's Guba that the Russian pauper turned into a Russian gentleman.

Kutepov himself, who, like everyone else, was paid two liras, is said to have procured a pair of good boots, his wife's dresses, and a sheath given by the regiment, while the general's pants were noticeably worn, but scrupulously clean.

He spoke rarely, and if he did, his words were simple and pure, like the beating of a strong heart. He used to say, "We are Russians, we are her last soldiers, and Russia awaits us." And in his simple and straightforward words of a simple man, Russian from head to

---

[3] "Oh, What Is This Night For?" and "I've Fallen in Love with a Damsel with All My Soul"

toe, everyone could hear the beating of their own heart.

He spoke rarely, but there was nothing this molten soldier wouldn't do. By order of his court, colonels were demoted to privates for drunkenness, and fifteen-days' arrest was imposed for an unstitched button or a torn pant leg. For him both officers and soldiers were equal, and he ruthlessly, without regard to their persons, washed away any dirt, any soot from the soldiers' honor. It was he who piled the dull strain of training, drills, marching, and saluting on the tired men. He is the one who saddled Gallipoli with the iron curb bit of iron discipline....

He did not prevent those who wanted to leave from doing so. The French herded people off to Brazil; the huge, smoky *Reshid-Pasha* repeatedly cut through the Gallipoli breakwater and called the Russians home, back to their homeland with a thick, hoarse hum.[4]

And some did leave. However, the general thought up a strange decree. All those who wished to leave the army could do so by declaring their resignation, within the following three days. But if you stay after the decree, it's final. You are a soldier, and any future resignations would be treated as betrayal, as fleeing from the line of battle.

Gallipoli paced and trotted under Kutepov's curb bit.

During the days of the decree about the freedom to resign from the army, there were some who thought that the whole army would flee given the opportunity. They said, "Who will be willing to continue eating canned beans and even eat, perhaps, scorpions?"

Kutepov only squinted his eyes, chuckling, "It's alright. It's necessary. We'll see."

---

[4] The *Reshid-Pasha* is a ship.

And only three out of thirty thousand resigned as refugees. His steel faith in the steel soldier triumphed.

And so Kutepov's orders fell on those who stayed. Tough orders, soldierly. If a man drank too much, made too much of a racket, he was sentenced to twenty to thirty days in the Guba. A young soldier snatched a can of condensed milk from some American boxes while on the clock—military prison.

Everyone knows the Guba. The Guba drew everyone in, even musicians who were too slow with the beat of the regimental march during parades. The army was drawn to the general's block; the army pulled up and stepped imperceptibly through the Guba, through its external displays of discipline, through the threat of martial punishment.

There are no Russian paupers, Russian thieves and robbers in Gallipoli. During the nine months of the Gallipoli stay there was only one robbery and two thefts. Kuzmin Karavayev, an old Russian lawyer, a connoisseur of laws and human crimes—when he was in Gallipoli—was surprised that, during the year of the army's stay, there was not a single crime against a woman's honor. The old lawyer said that in all armies there was an expected percentage of such crimes and that the Russian army was the only one where there hadn't been a single soldier who had offended a woman. . . .

And the old Turk, Muhmed-Ali, who peddles yellow English soap and Ottoman cigarettes by the harbor, rubbed his brown wrinkled fingers, rimmed with silver rings, against each other in front of me, and tried to tell me with his toothless, sunken mouth how good the Russian *kardesh* are.[5]

---

[5] Turkish for brother.

"I'm an old *asker*.[6] When your grand duke Prince Mikola went to take Istanbul, I was an *asker*. Then the French stayed here. Then the *Anglez* stayed here.[7] *Russ* no thief, *Russ* not *kulak*. *Russ* is good, *kardesh*, *Russ* like mullah."

Kutepov pushed the army hard, and only gradually, little by little, lowered the bar when they began to understand him, when even the impatient young lieutenants began to say that without Kutepov the army would have disintegrated into human rubble.

There was at first the following order: walking in the streets was allowed until seven o'clock in the evening, and anything later—to the Guba. Then it was permitted until nine, until ten, until eleven, now until twelve. In this way the general lowered the iron bridle.

And all went down the crooked curve of the faults of Guba's sitting occupants. Starting from robbery and theft, the Guba arrived to the days of its downfall, to drunkenness. A convoy-escort will rave in full strength, having received his lira for a month of soldierly hardship. A drunken military official will collapse into the dust in the middle of the street, singing a cruel romance in a hag's voice.... The Guba will take him.

They say that in the mornings at headquarters, Kutepov, signing orders for the corps, now sometimes asks the commandant, "So, how many do we have for the Guba? Many today.... Shall we put them in?"

And the army youths, laughing, talk about the following reliable omen: when the general wears the Drozdovtsy uniform, he is kind, no abuse, no hazing—a man without his suspenders still won't go to the Guba; when he wears the Kornilovtsy uniform,

---

[6] Turkish for soldier.
[7] The Englishmen.

anything can happen, both this and that; but when he wears Markovtsy epaulettes, he is sure to throw someone into the Guba.

Kutepych walks down the street: black gloves, in a black *gymnastyorka*.[8] He walks, striding firm and wide. Clean-shaven adjutants in dazzlingly white *gymnastyorki* stride beside him, gently jingling their spurs.

Brown Turkish girls scatter as a frightened flock of sparrows.

"Kutep-*Pasha*, Kutep-*Pasha*...."

The Senegalese sentries, who stand with their legs shoulder width apart by the houses over which fresh flags of the French Republic flutter in the blue sky, raise their rifles, which make short tinkles when discharged, and bare their teeth joyfully, keeping guard and saluting the Russian general in the Russian way, putting their parched and skinny palms to their temples. There never was an order for the Earrings to do so.

And yet they salute in this way out of heartfelt pleasure, just as they, with joyful passion, clicking their tongues and swiveling their eyes terribly, call Kutepov, "*Mon papa.... O, mon papa....*"

Kutep-Pasha squints his shiny, black eyes. He laughs. And everyone laughs, amused, at the Earrings' displays of respect.

This strong soldier, broad-boned, with a bald, steep forehead, was understood and respected in Gallipoli. In the Guba, dissatisfied with the customs of the army, the prisoners decided one day to hold an election for the corps commander. The election was conducted in accordance with all the rules—direct, anonymous, equal, and universal voting. Many generals' names were placed on the list. There were fifty men sitting in the Guba at that time, and when the papers were unfolded, all fifty votes were in favor of

---

[8] Russian military garment: pullover-style with a standing collar, double buttoned.

General Kutepov.

The stony, gray Guba, by which Russian sentries stand, is neither a dungeon nor a gloomy prison. In fact, it is something special, of Gallipoli, not seen anywhere else—it's simply the Guba. . . .

In the Guba, a garrison commander is chosen from among the prisoners, the senior in rank. He has his own adjutants, and he makes his own orders concerning the Guba.

The commandant of the city came one day to visit those arrested. He asked, "Do you have an old commander or a new one in your garrison?"

"A new one."

"And who is it?"

"Me."

"Well, greetings, boarders. . . ."

And in the evening the commander of the Guba garrison issues the following announcement: "On this day I took office as Commander of the Guba Garrison, and on this same day the Commandant of the City immediately paid me a visit, for which I tender him my thanks."

If there are a lot of arrestees, the Guba posts an announcement: "The manning of our garrison is going extremely well. I thank General Kutepov for constant reinforcement." In the Guba, the same discipline existed as beyond its walls. As soon as something is wrong the commander of the Guba garrison makes an announcement: "Today a lieutenant turned to a sentry for conversation. I reprimand the officer with a disciplinary offense: no talking to the sentries."

The Guba also has its own official seal: a lean, two-headed bird; one head is General Kutepov, and the other is the commandant of the city, and each clutches a small officer in its claw, dangling both his arms and legs. . . .

Kutepov visits the Guba on the eve of all major holidays, and "amnesty" is granted, and the Guba-sitters march, huddled, to the All-Night Vigil. . . .

The Guba also has its own poets. Some captain under long-term arrest composed an entire song. The verses are desperate, but it sings well, and the most important thing is that the whole song is permeated with the light of Gallipoli. . . .

The inmate sings about the stern and strict, kind-hearted and sensitive general, about his fight against corruption, slovenliness, soldier's drunkenness, against overall evil.

The inmate sings of how the general demanded order, how he strengthened the army's charters, how he worked day and night and thought of Russia.

He also sings of how the whole corps understood the general, how the White soldiers were cleansed of evil. And thus ends this song of the Gallipoli Guba:

"*Mistakes we shall not repeat;*
"*Our sins are clear to us.*
"*Toward feats our brothers we'll inspire*
"*And Russia'll become wonderful. . . .*"

They laugh good-naturedly at the Guba; they are not afraid of her; they even love her—as one of their own, as one of Gallipoli. Colonel Yakovlev, a small, skinny, very cheerful man and a local wit, who had fallen from vehicles many times, sings, with a broken nose, cheerful songs about the Guba at regimental outings.

There are caricatures of the Guba going around, just as there are of everything else. For example, the commandant of the city is depicted with his eyes bulging terribly, and his lip is huge, stretched, and sagging. And sitting on this monstrous lip are small officers, trembling like little mice. ... Kutepov has already collected a whole archive of caricatures of himself.[9]

At the *Ustnaya Gazeta* (Oral Newspaper) building, in the evening, the white-shirts slowly gather to listen to the lecturers, to merrily listen to newspaper fables. The lecturers, gaunt officers with glasses—who were students in the past, and quick-tongued, cleverly jingling their spurs, yesterday's newspaper-youth—report news from both *Novosti* (News) and *Volya* (Will), and excerpts from Soviet newspapers. These strange, open-air soldier's gatherings—which other army has them?

Ustnaya Gazeta is run by the black-eyed, already graying, but boyishly quick on his feet Reznichenko, a representative of the zemstvo-city organizations, shrewd in his work, quick on his feet in everything, hustling everything into the army—from faucets and sole leather to the latest Parisian publications; he was in love with the army like a sixth-grade gymnasium student.

Kutepov said that he only wants the truth, and the Gallipoli press decided to tell the truth. When all over the world Russian emigrants fell into a rosy hysteria at the frosty roar of cannons from the ports of Kronstadt, when politicians, like dazed gamblers, began to lay bets on the evolution of Bolshevism, on peasant uprisings, on famine, when the *Obshcheye Delo* (Common Cause) promised a mass exodus of commissars from the Kremlin in a fortnight, here, in the blue twilight, the gaunt, bespectacled lecturers, curling their stubby fingers, were firmly embossing: "Don't believe them. This is all either hysteria or fiction. Liberation won't come, neither today nor tomorrow. Strengthen your spirit. Don't believe them; they are blinded by political

---

[9] Guba in Russian means "lip," so the caricature is a play on words.

darkness. It's all self-deception over there, and the truth is simple: we are alone; we are semi-forgotten; and we must strengthen our spirit."

Besides the lively spoken press, there are a dozen of their own journals in Gallipoli. All of them are meticulously written on paper, with watercolors and pencil drawings carefully pasted on the pages. All these *Luchi (Rays of Light), Lepti artilleristov (The Artillerymen's Lepta), Sergievtsy, Razvey gore—v golom pole (Wade your cares away in the Bare Fields)* are somehow intimate. The journals are full of shy young people, memories, intimate and sad stories of young love, and good-natured caricatures of hunger strikes, discipline, and the Guba.

Language courses, gymnasiums, national universities, and libraries exist in Gallipoli, and quiet meetings are held there almost every evening. And they are also held in the town, where the Russian garrison theater has nestled on the mountain, near the brown ruins of an ancient amphitheater, and in the camps, where they have their own canvas theater stalls, from which the square benches of clay Russian amphitheaters, which were dug into the ground, fan upward.

In the evening, when the air begins to freshen, the dark Gallipoli resounds. A cornet draws a high velvety note somewhere. The sound of a soldier's prayer drifts in like a wave. The reflections of the cafes' lighted windows burn in the dark water, near the breakwater, like flickering pupils. The reflected light flutters like long, golden eyelashes.

Smooth sighs of copper trumpets can be heard—such smooth and tremulous sighs, like the flickering lights in the dark water at the breakwater. If you listen carefully, a quiet sadness can be heard, because the copper trumpets are playing old Russian waltzes and old overtures of Russian operas.

The wave of evening prayer, the resounding sadness of the copper, and lights, lights in the dark water....

Gallipoli resounds in the evening. In the garrison theater, "Na boykom meste" or maybe "Nora" or "Potonuvshiy kolokol" is playing.[10] In the brightest hall of Gallipoli, in a Greek club, where gas lamps burn, the Kornilovtsy or Alekseyevtsy regiment is giving a concert. All regiments have their own choirs, their own string orchestras. Russian music masters managed to make guitars and violins from the thin plywood of the canned food crates in the zemstvo workshops.

Gallipoli resounds....

In the barn, near the bazaar, in the central library, where, during the day, behind long plank-tables, the regulars rustled their pages in silence, coughing only a little—an art studio performs in the evening.

Under the flickers of candles, in the dark.... It's stuffy in the barn. The dark walls are dripping with sweat; the walls are wet as if from rain.

A bald, tall violinist is playing. Behind him, the little Yakovlev, grimacing affectionately, sings in a puny tenor a song about canned goods, about the Gallipoli Khaz-Bulat, who haggled a horse and a dagger for two lira, about Gallipoli's everyday life, about the Guba, beans, rumors....

The dark barn rumbles hotly and deeply with restrained laughter. On rickety Viennese chairs, in the first few rows, are Kutepov and his wife.

The chair beneath the general creaks firmly; Kutepov is laughing from his very gut. He laughs with a wide, soft crease on

---

[10] "At the Lively Place," "The Burrow," and "The Sunken Bell."

23

the back of his head and snorts with a wheeze, "Bravo, bravo...."

And on the narrow stage the white choir has already lined up. Everyone is white here, everyone in dazzling dandy shirts with long cuffs on the sleeves, as they wore in the army under Tsar Alexander III. At midday, when the sun hotly licks one's bronze back, I saw these shirts being washed on the shore of the sea....

The choir lined up. Candlelight from below illuminates the audience's faces, and their reflections glisten in the wide-open, dark eyes of the choir, as if tears had paused in the eyes of the singers.

They sing the "Chasovoy." The dark barn falls silent, having sighed in unison with the first exhale of the Kornilovtsy soldiers' song.

A sentry stands on watch. He is tired; he is hungry; he is alone.... "Do you hear, night, that I am alone?"

And the night answers with a deep breath, "I hear." And in its breath, distant echoes of "How Glorious" sing out, battle marches clatter vaguely, and the stirring rustle of old banners flows.

The sentry sings that he is hungry, tired, but he will not put his rifle down; he will not leave his post. "Do you hear, night?"

And the night answers with a deep breath, "I hear." And in response to her, the wind whispers in the expanse of the fields, the quiet hum of the belfries, the rustling of the croplands, and the singing of "How Glorious."

Kutepov's short, soldierly fingers roam, stroking his knees. In the stuffy barn there is a hot flutter of breath, and under its gust the candles flick yellow tongues, a wet glitter of candles in the dark eyes of the singers.

Outside, in the blue gloom, cigarettes flicker their red dots. Spurs jingle shyly and lightly. The white shirts are parting, slightly aglow.

I'm walking with Professor Davats. There was this private-docent of mathematics who came from Kharkov as a plain soldier to join the armored vehicle troop. Now he's an artillery lieutenant.

Davats is thin, with a narrow, pedigreed face and a graying, trimmed head, and he's wearing a baggy shirt. The common officers mock him good-naturedly: "He pulled the cord of a battle cannon once and died, mad with love for the army."

Davats is a quiet fanatic. He is like the priest of the army, and his military service is not service for him, but some kind of silent liturgy. He himself told me of how he had a headache once. It was unbearably painful, on that day, when General Wrangel arrived at our camp.

General Baron Pyotr Wrangel (1878–1928)

The day was dull and gray. Wrangel, tall and skinny as a pole, was walking up from the breakwater, and suddenly the sun broke through, illuminating the dust with the sun's gold.

"I took a look at the Commander-in-Chief and, you know, it was as if my headache had never even been there. . . ."

The professor takes off his glasses, and I see his eyes, blue, clear, moist, as if behind a transparent and light veil of tears. We walked on, talking in low voices.

"They call me a fanatic, an enthusiast. But I say that, just like everyone else, I have no enthusiasm."

Without enthusiasm, cursing, unbearably tired, they perform annoying tasks and work.

Without enthusiasm, perched on heaps of piled stones, on the scorched wastelands they call military schools, they sketch trajectories and projections on rusty pieces of iron.

And, of course, they read General Kutepov's new orders without enthusiasm. They do everything and endure everything, not because they are afraid of Kutepov, but because they want to continue and endure in this way. They know that only in this way and through this way will the army be kept alive; they know that only in this way will they carry their banners to Russia, through blood and fire, through defeats and victories. Such is their will: to endure in silence.

In the world beyond Gallipoli, no one suspects that in front of thousands of crowded soldiers, here, broken-up newspaper fables are being read. And who knows whether it was the headquarters, for its own aims, that painted a black X on Gallipoli rather than Paris or Prague.

"There they have taken a deceitful position; there they make the irreparable mistake of ignorance," Davats says to me quietly, rubbing his eyes with the palm of his hand. "They think that Gallipoli is built on deception and lies, but we are alive only with the inner awareness of our necessity, and we have neither lies nor deception, but truth and discipline."

I look sidelong at the slightly bulging, nearsighted eyes of the private-docent from the artillery. I remember his naive story about his headache and Wrangel.

Little is said about Wrangel in the army. Wrangel is outside the army, above it. Wrangel is not spoken of as a commander. For Gallipoli he is above a commander. Beyond the blue line of the sea, where the white paths of foam march in rows, languidly murmuring, there, in front of the whole world, Wrangel stands alone for Russia and her army.

Once, in the evening, two soldiers came up to me in the street. They were both elderly, dried out, and tanned to the black. One was blond and the other had a dark goatee. The light-haired one, wearing blue epaulettes with the white band of a sergeant, took a close look at my wrinkled, gray civilian suit and said timidly, "We want to ask you . . . did you arrive from Constantinople?"

"Yes."

"And so, how is it over there?"

"Well, not bad."

They stood around for a bit. The blond scratched the bridge of his nose and cleared his throat, as if about to confess something very intimate and therefore embarrassing.

"We know that it's bad over there.... And how is General Wrangel doing?"

"As far as I know, well, in good health."

"Well, maybe not. God grant him health ... because there've been rumors."

They saluted me and walked off together.

It is obvious that it is not only the Kharkov private-docent who is in love with Wrangel, and this shared feeling can't be called anything else but a soft and gentle love, which is reflected in their looks and smiles when they talk about Wrangel.... There is a narrow-gauge railroad in Gallipoli, laid by Russian hands from the camps to the city for the transportation of food. Two rusty strips of rail lay in the gray weeds, rolling over the sandy, sun-drenched slopes. The Russian builders chose the landscape profile well; low, creaky, and rusty wagon beds are pulled into the camps by horses, and from the camps the wagon beds run themselves down the slope. Often, however, they run so fast that they spin off the rails....

Wrangel's wife had visited the camps. She's thin, like an English miss, very cheerful and lively, with a sparkling white smile. She was traveling by wagon-carriage. On the narrow-gauge

Mrs. Olga Wrangel visiting the camps, pictured right of center

railway, where there are Drozdovtsy and Kornilovtsy camping lots in the bare fields, there are dedicated station commandants. One of them, right before the city, when the carriages had stalled, reported to the chief of traffic, "I have the honor to report that, in the area entrusted to me, there have been no incid—"

The baroness effortlessly jumped off the wagon bed and, laughing, looked up and down the young officer.

"Bite your tongue. Just before your station our train suffered a derailment: the carriage overturned."

They tell of this incident with a joyful smirk, as if in love.

The army loves Wrangel. The army knows that Wrangel is its lone wall before the entire world.

And the broad-shouldered and tough Kutep-Pasha is within the army itself. He is its tooth and nail, its tough and strong cement.

They're not in love with Kutep-Pasha, but Kutep-Pasha is now understood and firmly respected. In Gallipoli they understand that Kutep-Pasha is not an autocrat or an executioner, but a loyal, unyielding Russian soldier.

He clenches his iron glove firmly. When he thinks something over and executes it, it's over.

He has a beveled, wrathful forehead, squinted, intense eyes, and an awkward but supple gait. This is a strong man who knows no doubts. He does not like words, because he considers words to be lies and the pastime of chatterboxes.

He thinks, most likely, that Russia needs a tall guardsman in a bear hat more than she needs chatterboxes from the benches of the Convention.

He marched through blood. He marched just as stubbornly and briskly through attacks, under fire. He hacks into pieces. He's not afraid of the gallows. He won't abolish the death penalty during wartime.

He is a molded and resolute soldier, of the kind of molded soldiers who shape human history. Behind him lies the blaze of fires, the black snakes of assault formations, and the rumble of cannonades and bells. . . .

He is always calm and always a little mocking. And his mocking has a lot of soldierly, tough grit to it.

One day, a French representative suddenly officially informed General Kutepov that he should not worry if French troops were to be engaged in practice maneuvers. The general officially replied, "I do not worry, but there is an extraordinary coincidence: I will also be carrying out the practice of maneuvers in combat gear tomorrow; you don't worry either."

And so the next day the Gallipoli Junkers' College and the technical regiment embarked for their exercises with rifles and machine guns. Kutepov stands by his words. Everyone knows this.

Students of the Gallipoli Junkers College, 1921

During the roughest days of Gallipoli, during the days of Brazilian promises, during the days when the horn of the *Reshid-Pasha* beckoned homeward, during the days when the black children of the wonderful French Republic posted decrees that Russian soldiers should disobey their commanders, and during the days of the decree of being able to leave for all those who wished to, Kutep-Pasha remained calm and a little mocking.

His short, soldierly fingers quiver slightly, and he pales with worry, drawing in air deeply through his flared nostrils, only when tattered, rolled-up Russian banners pass in front of him.

He sits there now, too, the stern Kutep-Pasha, up at the top, in a small, cabin-like staff waiting room, where one has to climb to, up a steep, freshly carved ladder, and, perhaps, while signing an order, squints his intense, black eyes at the commandant: "How many do you have for the Guba? Well, let's put them in...."

General Kutepov overseeing the exercises of a training regiment, 1921

White Birds

Heat.

The sky was enveloped in a dark smoke of heat. If only a cloud would flicker like white fluff in the merciless, burning desert of the sky.

By the gray, low house of the Russian Headquarters, where violet, hectograph-printed orders and warped sheets of the *Obshcheye Delo (Common Cause)*, yellowed by the heat, are pasted on the walls, a bunch of white shirts are silently tramping about. Their boots are dusty. The sweat-slicked shirts stick to their backs with dark, wet spots on their shoulder blades. They read the newspapers in silence. They stare at the lines with a tired, dark, and heavy gaze.

A mute heat. Gallipoli has turned white under the sky-blue desert. A cloud of dust is blowing along the white street near the headquarters. Soldiers are returning from work: they were unloading French canned goods at the port.

Their boot-wrappings are covered with dust, and their shirts are unbuttoned at the collar. They walk, stomping their feet deafly and in unison, and kick up lazy, gray streams of dust, like a herd.

All their faces are dry, dark with tan, and their eyes are dark and tired. Their tin flasks clink with every step: "We are tired.... Tired.... Tired...."

Dark fatigue in every gaze. There is no loud laughter here. There is no loud talking, no shouting, no curses ringing like slaps.

Weathered, brown faces, covered in glossy skin, and a hot weariness in their gaze. They are very tired. They are warriors: they lived like players at a crazy card table where death set the stakes. They lived as in a hazy masquerade, as in a diabolical panorama, where the boulevards of the cities, the rumbling train stations, the "Teplushka" train wagons, the villages, the wire fences, the wet fields all flew by in a galloping confusion.... Over mountains, over valleys—here today, there tomorrow.

Orel, Kiev, Novorossiysk, Rostov, Tsaritsyn, Kharkov, Simferopol. Overturned, torn-up cannons. Red wagons shattered into splinters. Black-red clouds of fires, hanging over steppe villages. A pulp of human flesh in the coal pits of steamship holds.... Here today—there tomorrow.

And behold, as if Joshua had suddenly ordered the sun to rise, it was one long, scorching day. The sun never sets again. No more dawn. The blue desert of the sky, the white dust, and the harrowing noise of white foam in the blue desert of the sea.

But this will pass, this: Kutepov's orders, disgusting outfits, gray canned food with worms and black chowder and stinging dust and famished longing and the dry half-whisper, half-whistle of burned-out thorny burdock....

This will soon pass, tomorrow this will pass. They will go to Russia; the generals promised them two months. They will go to Batumi, march to Serbia, to Bulgaria, to Siberia. The orchestras, glittering with joy, will strike the marching tune.... But the scorching day stands still. And the scorching day stands for a month and two months and half a year. There's no tomorrow. The sun doesn't set anymore. No fresh dawn sounds.

"We are tired.... Tired.... Tired...." clink the soldiers' flasks. "But we wait, we wait, we wait."

The soldiers passed, kicking up a canopy of dust behind them like a herd.

Two lop-eared donkeys are walking, sleepily swaying their white-haired gray muzzles. They carry long poles, between which a canvas hammock sways slightly. One donkey is being smacked with a stick on its thick, scrawny behind by a Sister of Charity— white, plain-haired, and wearing worn-out shoes on a bare foot. Slowly, swaying, with their ears pricking and their little hoofs treading lightly, the donkeys are diligently carrying the hammock. Beneath the white sheet stretched a narrow body with a sunken belly. The sun burns an oily and dull spot on its bronze forehead. Probably typhoid....

Dysentery spreads in the white camps. Typhoid fever has risen from the dry and clayey camp river and is marching through the tents of the Russian Guards. Mosquito fever, a fierce Gallipolytic fever, throws people instantly to their bunks. People burn; their darkened lips dry up. The dark smoke of heat in their eyes. People do not survive typhus. Those seized by the epidemic burn up instantly without strength, without a fight. Tuberculosis roams through the camps.

There are no cases of the Russian rash because there are no lice here. Everyone maintains cleanliness, their undergarments washed as if by an expert laundress. When Kutepov visits a regiment or a school, he often has such conversations with the Junkers and soldiers:

"Take off your *gymnastyorka*.... Show me your underpants, your shirt.... Good, clean. And now unfasten your wrappings; show me your shoelaces...."

They clean. They wash. And there are no Russian lice here.

But the camps are tired of fevers; the camps are starving. Nine months of slow, grim hunger. Every day aspic-gray, rigid tins of canned food and black chowder in which you can count fifty pieces of swollen watery beans. The whole day's ration can be grasped in one handful. It is said that a special commission of foreign doctors examined the ration and found it too little for a grown man for one day:

Bread: up to 1 pound.

Grain: 1/4 pound.

Canned goods: 5/8 pound.

Fats, sugar, salt: 1/20 pound of each.

There isn't enough bread. When it is cut into five or six, one man lies down on his bunk and turns his back to the wall, and they ask him, "For whom?"

Closing his eyes, he calls the names. The bread is shared equally, evenly, and the lucky one gets an extra piece after a hungry draw of the straw.

The day is planned out. Hours of exercises go by, and the people who are free from them lie naked, from the morning, on the white-hot sand by the sea. People charred by the sun lie in some kind of dark-golden tangled pattern on the white shore. Bathers swim and dive like seals, sending out a dazzling glitter of splashes. You lie there, with stretched out arms and legs. The sun licks your body with hot tongues. The midday horn coos sadly in the barracks of the Senegalese. You look, sleepily, through the solar stupor, as the dark sea sways behind the white wall of sand, as bathers shine with splashes, you look at these tall, dark, sun-gilded people and remember that they are all Russians, they are all grandsons of the Sun. . . .

And a hot slumber swaddles us. In the morning, when they are free from their work and attire, they lie on the white shore. In this hot slumber the day passes like a dream, and no hunger is to be felt in this solar stupor. And you keep lying there due to the hunger, so that in the evening you instantly swallow your rations, which can be grasped in one single handful.

We wanted to catch fish in groups for the army cauldron, but France banned fishing these waters. My teeth can no longer chew pulpy canned food, and it is nauseating to chug the dark, hot water with swollen beans. Nauseating.

There is a hungry scurvy in the camps. Russian children and women are barefoot, and their legs are often wrapped at the ankles with gauze bandages. On their bronze backs, on their arms, on their legs, there are blue, wide welts, like spots of bedsores. Why? They say it's saltpeter. There is saltpeter in the canned food, and it causes these saltpeter spots.

"We eat saltpeter." That's what they say in Gallipoli.

It's easier for the boys and the married men. Reznichenko, the lively on his feet, black-eyed, fast-paced zemstvo-city representative, feeds lunches to the weak and feeble, giving out more than 120,000 lunches in six months of work in four "feederies." Near the harbor, in a narrow alley, in a dusty, box-strewn shed, a small, burned-out, starry American flag is nailed to the wall, and a kindly, starry man walks there with his hands in his pockets. The tall man, that shaven and gaunt American captain, twitching his left leg, probably shot somewhere, is always cheerful and always whistling.

Woolen blankets, bombazine pajamas, fluffy vests, scarves, sweet milk, some strange Canadian pâté, playing cards, and even shaving cream are finding their way into the camp on behalf of the starry man.

What cannot be eaten, they distribute to the Greeks in exchange for tomatoes, melons, and bread. The towering man knows this, but only whistles merrily, with his hands deep in his pants pockets, long, hairy hands, like hairy shafts.

There's nothing to add to the rations, unless they go out in the evening with fishing rods onto the rocks to catch silver mackerel and mullet; unless they make coal and sell a sack of it in town for five to six drachmas. The price of coal in Gallipoli has fallen greatly.... They make coal in the black bushes about eight miles from the camps. In the heat they scorch their faces over the fires and scratch their hands bloody on the thorny bushes. And in the heat, tired and black as devils from the firepits, they pull sacks eight miles away to the bazaar. And before that, perhaps, they'd spend the whole night on duty and, sleepless, they'd then go to cut wood....

They don't speak of hunger in Gallipoli. They don't want to admit that they are hungry, and if you ask them, they will say, "Yes, we're a bit hungry, of course, but more so it's all just very monotonous...."

They make fun of the hunger, just as they do of the Guba. There's even a song:

"*Under the sultry skies of Gallipoli,*
"*Where the camps are whitening in the field,*
"*All the men are swollen with beans.*"

And when rumors circulated in Gallipoli that no rations would be provided at all, everyone became sort of cheerful and curious:

"I wonder what will come out of this?"

They strode through the hunger as well, just as they strode through the Guba, through the iron block and the iron gloves of discipline.

And when they heard in Gallipoli that Russia was starving, when telegrams about millions of crowds displaced by hunger from the Volga region came rushing in, as if by common consensus, all regiments and batteries decided to give their one-day Gallipoli rations to hungry Russia, given to her from her Russian White camps.

The road to the camps from the headquarters is straight, through golden scorched fields, past the windmills, along the stony shore where the Dardanelles' skyline looms, lower and lower into the brown, narrow valley, above which the brooding mountains shift with a blue, undulating border.

A gray path winds through the valley along a heat-soaked river. This is the Valley of Roses and Death; these are the Gallipoli camps.

Long, white rows of tents. Just like white birds lying in rows next to each other, having folded their white wings.

In the canvas walls of the tents are small windows with a canvas frame, crosswise. In front of the tents were carefully trampled, narrow paths, sandy squares of plazas, dusty, burned-out flower beds on stone lawns, and gray regimental monograms and two-headed eagles made of sea pebbles. Far away, between the white tents, the round, bulbous onion domes of the regimental church of the Guards Artillery stand darkly green. The green church, made of heather and plane trees, has already turned yellow, is already withering and crumbling, but the Russian onion domes are still so green and so joyful in the blue above the white tents.

Behind the gray river, above the precipice, there is a stake-shaped building of the corps theater, where Sunday camp meetings are held.

Markovtsy in their tent, 1921

A lonely, ancient, and silent sycamore tree stands on the valley like a sentry, having scattered a heavy bowl of branches near General Vitkovsky's tent. And, all around, white churches, white theaters, white soldier's houses stretch out. The Whites are stretching across the river, pushing into the blue mountains. White birds lay down right beside one another in the valley, having folded their white wings.

A strange architect has built a strange city in the Valley of Roses and Death. White soldiers live beneath the white birds: artillery and infantry, the Young Guards, the Drozdovtsy, the Kornilovtsy, the Markovtsy and Alekseyevtsy, and the joint Guards battalion of the old St. Petersburg Semyonontsy, Izmailovtsy, and Pavlovtsy.[11]

And beyond the river, by the velvety blue mountains, sleep the white birdhouses of the Russian cavalry.

A quiet town in a valley where thirty thousand people live and breathe. A ghostly Russian city by the blue Gallipoli mountains.

All along the tents, along the front row, on a narrow yellow path, poles were dug in, covered with straw, like light straw umbrellas. These are the stations of the regimental sentries.

All along the tents, beyond the front row, there are more straw tents on yellow broom-scratched patches of ground. Golden wheat is laid between four tall poles. The long, brittle ends sway slightly, rustle, and under the straw tents, in the shade, Russian banners, wrapped in their covers, sleep, propped up against the walls.

Banners of the young Drozdovtsy and of the Kornilovtsy, and regimental banners of the Russian Guards. Faded scraps of brocade are on the shafts, and dull banner tassels hang downwards, flowing gravely along the shafts.

Sentries stand an unbroken guard, night and day, by Russia's sleeping banners. . . .

A silver half-light in the regimental canvas churches. A clay floor, tin chandeliers made of cans, a lectern covered with a red-stitched village towel. From the low and squat altar doors, the saints look out. The gray curls of their beards and halos glow with

---

[11] Regiments are usually named after their leader.

silver. Their eyes are huge, blue and gaze luminous and sad.

The Archangel Gabriel is on the altar doors, wearing a scarlet cloak and carrying a white lily, while the angel's face is pale and austere and the wind blows back the chestnut curls from his fair forehead.

You open the altar door, and behind it there are chopped boards from the canned food crates, a subframe onto which a brown canvas from a sack was stretched by an unknown and tender artist. Black French letters, "S.—O.", still remain on the canvas, as well as a long number: 48352....

The half-light is silvery in the regimental tents too. Bunks made of brownish shrubbery are lined with gray blankets. By the bunks are makeshift tables and flimsy planks of shelves. And around each tent there is always a path, as straight as a taut string, sprinkled with yellow sand.

Officers and soldiers sleep together in the white tents, bunk to bunk. There's the same black chowder and gray canned food for everyone in the white tents. The Kornilovtsy invite the soldiers to their officers' meeting on Sundays. On the soccer field, where groans resound on the days of regimental matches, the generals kick a leather ball around with the soldiers. In this city of white birds, by the wheat patches, where the guards stand an unbroken guard by the banners, everything proceeds quietly and with a unique calmness.

Soldiers, in white shirts with red epaulettes and white caps like the kind worn in Skobelev's time;[12] non-commissioned officers of older periods of service; snub-nosed young men; gray-haired Guardsmen who still remember Tsar Alexander III; officers; thin

---

[12] Mikhail Skobelev, a general famous for his heroism in the 1877–8 Russo-Turkish War.

St. Petersburg Guardsmen; Kharkov gymnasium students; clerks from Kiev; students from Rostov; Russian aristocrats; and mustached Russian Wachtmeisters from Kaluga's stock of peasants, who had been promoted to lieutenants and colonels. They live together. They eat together. They think together. They know every gesture, every habit of their neighbor. They know each other to the core, to the last nerve. And each has a part of the other. They have communion with one another. They breathe as one.

They would have split up. They would have scattered, gone in droves to Brazil, to Argentina, to Sovietdom,[13] anywhere, to Hell, if their forever silently-accepted Gallipoli communion had not merged them into one.

In the white city of birds there are no Kaluga peasants, no Ivanovs and Petrovs, no yesterday's Red Army soldiers from Orel and volunteers from Tsaritsyn, no hussars, no gymnasium teachers or clerks. There are only White soldiers in the white city. They are soldiers; they are the Drozdovtsy and the Markovtsy, guardsmen and cavalrymen, generals and lieutenants, bombardiers and corporals. They are White soldiers; they are not peasants or boyars; they are not refugees or emigrants.

They are Russian soldiers, and they await the coming of Russia.

They know that Russia is coming, and so they wait and stand an unbroken guard at its folded banners.

Silence in the white city.... Everyone's eyes are sad and bright, like those of the saints on the altar's panels. And in their speech and in their manners they all have a special, sensitive politeness. Such a quiet and gentle politeness can be found in very intelligent people and also in monks.

---

[13] In Russian *Sovdepia*, a derogatory term for the Soviet Union.

"It's strange and wonderful here," my interlocutor, a gaunt, freckled colonel with red, furrowed eyebrows, says to me.

We stand together by a small window in General Vitkovsky's tent.

"I came here from Greece," says the general. "There, like everyone else, I thought that the army was gone, that it was dead, but here I saw something new and terrible. I can't yet understand what it is.... In Gallipoli there is some kind of mobilization of the human spirit. There is one idea here: Russia is alive; Russia is not dead; Russia will always exist; and we, Russian soldiers, must serve her wherever our regiments may stand, in Gallipoli, in Bulgaria, in Africa. If you have enough spirit, serve; this means you are a Russian soldier. And they serve. I look at them, and it's wonderful, and strange. Well, we, the officers, are understandable, but there are these soldiers, this Red Army darkness of yesterday. I don't recognize them. There were no such people under the tsar, or during the Revolution, or in the Civil War. How can I make myself clear to you.... Well, at least recall the Russian encampments, recall the Russian trenches, always covered with filth to the brim. But here they look after themselves particularly carefully; they seek cleanliness; they've built washrooms. There is a puritanical purity of morals here. Below the camps, in a tent, lives a prostitute, a fat Greek woman. Every day the Senegalese come to see her. And our guys don't go to her, nobody; they spit at the idea. Look at how snow-white and clean their shirts are. They're seeking cleanliness. Their soul is bare, a clean soul.... Well, take for example the fact that we don't hear any Russian swearing or profanity. Look at how they pray in church, how they listen to the spoken newspapers. They live with one single thought: Russia is alive and Russia will always exist, and they must serve her, because she is alive and because she will always exist. There are thirty thousand of us, without even a handful of soil from our homeland, and we have our old banners and our old commanders. And I keep wondering what to compare us to. Military history has never known such an army . . . except perhaps the stern and quiet regiments of Oliver Cromwell."

I look through the low window at the flat wasteland of the valley, where light rows of birds run white up to the blue mountains. And for a moment it seems to me that I am dreaming. And in my dream I see White Russian camps, maybe of the Sevastopol defense, maybe on the wastelands of San Stefano, maybe near Geok Tepe.

The half-light was silvery in General Vitkovsky's tent too. As you enter: a plank table where military maps and green work files are laid out, and behind a white curtain another plank table—this is the general's dining room. On the linen wall there is an image: a gray-haired saint in crimson robes with a blue omophorion.

General Vitkovsky, a short man of soft gait, with small, white hands covered in light twigs of blue veins. He had a graying, russet head, and his round chin was shaved down to blue, and his eyes were bright and steely, with white blades of cold pupils. And from his face, and from his soft gait, and from his white hands, a smell of monastic cleanliness emanates.

General Vitkovsky, whose cold fearlessness and leisurely walks under direct fire are known to the whole army, drinks yellow tea in quiet sips from a white, fragile cup. He drinks tea with dried prunes and says to me softly, "Put it inside the cup. It tastes better. And it helps with the stomach."

The fearless general, a cold daredevil, moves a saucer of prunes toward me with his white hand and gently keeps the conversation going.

"I still haven't been to Constantinople. And I don't have any desire to go there either."

In the white silence of the tent I feel exactly as if I were in a white monastery cell. And just like this, a long time ago, in our northern monastery, I was gently treated to prunes by a soft, quiet monk.

I look at the general's small, almost feminine fingers, and it appears to me that at dusk, when the evening's dawn is sung, he whispers intimate prayers to his saint in crimson robes with a blue omophorion, and crosses his chest quickly with timid, light crosses. I think that, like him, the quiet captains of the Long Parliament and of the Lord Protector Oliver Cromwell, who are of monastic cleanliness, went into the fire with their biblical regiments of round-headed Puritans who carried the Psalms under their leather coats.

By the general's tent, under a dark plane tree, stands a sentry with his sword unsheathed. And when the general comes out, the sentry jerks his shoulder and the saber instantly flashes its light, then dims out.

Above the velvety blue of the mountains, the sunset's scarlet ocean burns out in golden smoke. The fiery spears of the sun fade. The hulks of the cloud towers crumble. A blue evening silence rises higher and higher, like a tide, from the blue mountains into the sunset's scarlet ocean.

A trumpeter sings the evening's dawn.

I see him. He stands far, a blue shadow. The sunset's gold glows on the copper of the trumpet. The trumpeter sings the evening's dawn, raising his trumpet high, toward the four corners of the world.

The dawn calls for someone from beyond the mountains, from the evening's smoky distance. It rises with short cries, like a bird beating its scarlet wings, eager to fly into the sunset.

I see it clearly, the blue shadow of the trumpeter, scarlet blazing on the copper. And I don't know what the blue trumpeter is singing about or whom he is calling for from across the entire world. I walk quietly to the white tents of the Drozdovtsy. In front of me, my long, evening shadow moves along the sand of the path.

In the tent of the young generals, Manstein and Turkul,[14] there is a gray half-light. The tent is deeply dug into the clay earth, and one has to descend three or four earthen steps. The tent has the damp chill of a cellar.

There's a planked, uncovered, and long table along the tent, like a funeral home. In the middle of it, out of a circular slit in the board, a brown pole protrudes, which holds up the tent.

The tent of the young generals is like a cold cell, like a casemate, where they write short, yearning lines on the walls, where they cut and scratch monograms of names, prayers, and curses into the stone. . . . I have a silent heaviness in my soul. It seems to me that under this gray, cold tent, lying low to the ground, bound birds, proud and fearful, are pounding about.

---

[14] Vladimir Manstein, known as the "One-Armed/Armless Devil," was a legendary "exterminator of commissars," known for his bloodlust when it came to Bolsheviks. Unfortunately, his child had died in Gallipoli, and being unable to adjust to civilian life after the Drozdovtsy regiment left Gallipoli for Sofia, Bulgaria, he shot himself and his wife in a park, in 1928. Anton Turkul, an officer under Drozdovsky (while he was still alive) and later the chief of this same regiment, undertook many anti-Communist activities in the interwar period and eventually joined Vlasov's Army (Russian collaborationist formation fighting under Germany); he was arrested following the Second World War and detained for two years, after which he continued his life and political activity in Munich, passing away in 1958.

General Turkul is sitting by the table with one foot over the other. His tall and soft officer's shins gleam slightly. His broad chest is covered with a dark *gymnastyorka*. The general is narrow in the waist. His long, strong fingers, encrusted with gold rings, crumple a cigarette nervously and sprinkle yellow stringy tobacco on the table.

Turkul is about twenty-five years old, and he resembles all the Kornilovtsy and Drozdovtsy: always gaunt, black-haired, and dark-eyed. Turkul has a small, finely combed, shapely head, a narrow nose with a hump, and a black string of whiskers above a young mouth with dried lips. He sits with his head tilted back, and in the gray half-light his mouth is a little open, and the gold filling of a tooth gleams faintly.

I watch how he laughs, which causes deep, black wrinkles to run down from the inflated wings of his nose to his lips. I watch how he spits simply and noisily, in a soldierly manner. I look into his eyes. Their color is elusive, brown-gray with an iron tint. And I feel a shaky, glass wall between his eyes and mine.

General Manstein rests his chin on his hand. He has no other arm, up to the shoulder. The general's epaulet hangs by one button.

Manstein is a reddish brown-haired man. He is about twenty-eight years old. His face is shaved like an actor's. His black eyebrows are raised in a painful, Garshin-like way, and it seems to me that his young face is like the tragic mask of all the untold sufferings of the White Army.... He had lifted his tired eyes from his dilapidated Book of Genesis, and an unspoken sadness was burning in his suffering gaze.

Turkul speaks with a provincial vernacular. He says "vYsoko" instead of "vysokO" (high). He spits through his teeth onto the

General Anton Turkul (1892–1957)   General Vladmir Manstein (1894–1928)

earthen floor. Shapely and jovial, he resembles a rude Junker. He looks like a provincial seminarian who has been promoted to warrant officer.

General Turkul and General Manstein are the most terrifying soldiers of a most terrifying civil war. General Turkul and General Manstein are the wild madness of the Drozdovtsy's attacks at their fullest potential without ever firing a single shot; they are the mute frenzy of the invincible Drozdovtsy's marches. Generals Turkul and Manstein are merciless mass shootings, rags of bloody flesh and chins split open by the blued hilt of a Nagant, and cinders of raging fires, a whirlwind of madness, graveyards, death, and victories.

Generals Turkul and Manstein are the inhuman fearlessness of brave men, the myth of the Drozdovtsy: that war heroes were executed over a peasant's stolen chicken, that they walked under machine gun fire without crouching, that they swept away entire Red divisions with simple overnight advances and instantaneous attacks.

Turkul and Manstein are the heroic and fatal flight of the White Army, the flight of a wounded eagle, doomed to death.

Turkul and Manstein are the mythical defense of the Crimea: a line of fire, a line of blood, of retreats into a blinding blizzard, of swift attacks, of falls, of summits, of a pitiless struggle to the end, to the last clip, to the last breath, to the last death rattle.

Turkul and Manstein are officer-boys. And maybe Turkul is no more than a provincial seminarian thrown into the heat of revolutionary warfare, who rose to the scale of a historical hero, a legendary soldier, a living myth of the White War.

Manstein raises his narrow eyebrows in sorrow. . . . Manstein is the Armless Devil, cold as a machine, an exterminator of commissars. Manstein is a heroic legend of the White Army. Manstein is a terrifying fantasy of fire, death, and blood. Manstein is the breath, the heart, the rhythm of the White Army.

Manstein is a skinny, clean-shaven officer, an infantry lieutenant-boy, the kind of men who die without a cry, without a name, without a trace, in their very first battle, chuckling inspiringly and joyfully at their own young death. They die among millions of others who are just as traceless, for whom history leaves not even a speck of honor on its pages.

Manstein, the clean-shaven, armless infantry lieutenant, did not die, by chance, in his first battle. And then, in all his battles, history preserved him for itself, saved him, chose him out of the millions of the traceless—as a symbol, as a branded chosen one and a personal favorite.

Also, General Denikin promoted Manstein's father, an old

I V A N   L U K A S H

Army colonel, a kind man, and a kind conversationalist over a glass of good old wine, to the rank of general. He promoted him to general "for the heroic deeds of his son."

Old Manstein followed his son into battle and handed him machine-gun belts under fire. The son and father often sat in bivouacs sharing a bottle of wine. Another Manstein also went into battle: a young cadet, the grandson of Old Manstein through another son.

In one battle, the grandson was wounded. He fell down, quivering in pain, and then crawled to his grandfather and began to call out to him through clenched teeth, "Grandpa, do you hear me? I'm wounded."

Old Manstein pulled him up on his tachanka, laid him down on its straw, covered him with his overcoat, and said, stroking his hot teenage head, "Good, that you're wounded. That's how it should be, that you're wounded. And it doesn't matter that it hurts. Bear through it, soldier...."

General Manstein raised his thin eyebrows, contracted them in a sorrowful crease, and looked over my head, out the high window into the distance. He was definitely not listening to what Turkul was saying.

"I remember our attack on a Red Tatar regiment," Turkul recounts. "We got up, stood up, and advanced without firing a single shot. The Tatars had been lying in wait at a station.... Our attacks were always met with random fire. The machine guns whipped at us, but we marched on and knew they couldn't withstand our steady stride and our silence. And here we were, walking, and we met with silence. As we approach: silence.... Some began to slow their pace; some, worrying, started to hurry. Everyone is worried. Silence.... We're walking without a

51

sound. . . . And in that moment, when maybe we would not have endured the silence any longer and would have rushed back, the Tatars got up; they were waving their arms, sticking their bayonets into the ground. And not even shouting, but sort of squealing with fear. . . . Then we overran their entire regiment."

"Do you remember how we captured those cadets?" Manstein turns his thin eyebrow toward Turkul.

"You bet," says Turkul and clears his throat. "We didn't spare them. But they themselves didn't ask for mercy either."

"They fought very well," Manstein intervenes softly, stammering and choosing his words carefully. "There were many former cadets among their officers. Cadets from the cadet corps became Red officers, as one would go to a Junker school. And there were Communist boys too. One, I remember, was led to be executed, and he was laughing and singing 'Vstavay, prokliatyem zakleymyonniy.'"[15]

Manstein went into thought again, and his face softened.

"You know, we had to execute many men," Turkul says. "I have whole companies of captured Red Army soldiers in my regiment. We had to screen them mercilessly. You line up the prisoners and ask: 'Are there any Communists?' They don't say a word. You approach the first one: 'Are there any Communists?' He answers, 'There are none.' 'Execute him.' They'll take him away and execute him. You ask the next one, 'Are there any?'—'Yes, there are.'—'Who?'—'That one,' and others shout, 'And that one. And that son of a bitch too. . . .' Up to ten Communists per every hundred prisoners had to be executed. The rest became beautiful, fearless, iron soldiers. . . ."

I look at Turkul. There's a glass, shaky wall between him and I,

---

[15] "Arise, [you] curse-branded."

an invisible wall between us.... A drench of blood, corpse fumes, petrified dead men's hands, splattered with the yellowish jelly of brains. This black-haired, narrow-waisted young man is war as it is, as it will always be. A war without rose-colored verbiage and without any white gloves. Not the kisses of the perfumed Arcadian Shepherds nor the game of toy soldiers—human warfare, a rattling beast. This black-haired boy is the spawn of clangorous death, of the roar of fires, of the shriek of gunfire, and of the fury of the rattling attack marches. He is a man of another caliber, of another dimension of life. He speaks calmly, without hurry, and his mouth is slightly ajar, and for some reason his gold filling, which glistens dimly in the gray twilight, weighs on me.

Manstein lightly turns a sorrowfully raised eyebrow at me and suddenly smiles softly and gingerly.

"Yes, a lot of death. Lots and lots of death.... And, you know, they all die in silence. You put them in front of rifles and they just clam up, without a sound. Pale and downcast. And they don't cross themselves."

"Only—how should I put it?—the intellectuals, I guess, asked for mercy," adds Turkul. "Various Red commanders and various political agents. They humiliated themselves disgustingly. They licked our boots. They called us 'Your High Excellency.'"

"Yes," Manstein softly agrees. "Except for those, they all die silently, resignedly. And I don't know why they die like that. They've gotten used to death over the past few years...."

The generals reminisce.... They reminisce about how they almost captured the legendary commander of the Red Cavalry, Gai, a Kalmyk Cossack Wachtmeister. Gai escaped, and his car and his chauffeur were taken by the Drozdovtsy. The chauffeur—

who knows, maybe a Communist—became the generals' chauffeur and often drove them alone at night along unknown field roads. In Sevastopol, when we were evacuating, the chauffeur asked permission to stay behind, and it was granted. . . .

General Turkul lights a cigarette and clears his throat.

"There, and now we're staying here. But I know that as soon as they hear the command to set out, everyone will get up and go. Everyone is waiting in suspense to get going. There are even some who can't bear it. Eight officers in my regiment shot themselves. All good officers. And not because life was bad, or because life was poor or boring, but because they longed for their native land. They couldn't bear the longing."

They shot themselves because they couldn't bear the strain. Their souls burst. The army is activity; it is movement and combat, not confined stay at camp. People from the army, soldiers, officers, for years, from one day to the next, threw their lives to death as a wager. And in return for such a wager they demanded their life to its fullest; they took life feverishly and impetuously. And if the confined immobility of anticipation could still be tolerated by an inactive civilian, what strength of soul must be gathered, to what height of strained spirit must these active men—these men who exchanged their lives for death every day, these men from the Army who are now confined in Gallipoli—rise?

Turkul is talking about suicides, and for some reason I am reminded of that young officer of the Guards whom I met yesterday in a Gallipoli coffee house. The Guardsman spoke to me, clinking his long, sharpened little-finger nail against the rim of a glass:

"I often think of St. Petersburg. Suddenly, without any reason.

Suddenly the embankments float in my eyes, some street on the St. Petersburg coast that I've already forgotten the name of. And suddenly you want a glass of good old wine, the fine smell of perfume, to the point of acute pain. It's scary. These are all imperceptible trials. It's the past. And it takes a lot of strength not to think, a lot of strength.... But we've left the past. In Gallipoli, the fog of the Civil War washed off us; the past died. We are kind of bare here. We are neither the old Tsarist army nor the Civil War army. We are new. We live with one bare pain, that our dear Russia is gone, but that it will be there eventually; we don't know what kind of Russia, but not the dead one we have today...."

"Everyone is so tense," said Turkul, taking a deep puff of his cigarette, "so tense that we almost ought to march on Constantinople. After all, we could take it and, having seized whatever ships we could find, return to Russia. We await our peaceful home; we await Russia."

General Manstein raises his narrow eyebrows lightly and sorrowfully and looks far away, past us, into the vastness.

"Yes, Russia is awaited...."

And their souls are heated to the core, by the motionless anticipation. And some of them burst, and others harden like unbending steel.... They say that not long ago, when everyone knew that the Gallipoli sit-down was over, when they knew that the army would be advanced to the Balkans, the Junkers of one of the schools, those hairless, fit, healthy, strong, tanned Kutepov-lads, suddenly began to dig their dugouts for a winter campsite, but Kutepov forbade this with a special decree.

The tanned, white-toothed youth, these Russian gymnasium pupils, realists, students, who came out of the blast furnace of battle, are afraid of neither winter, nor hunger, nor homesickness, nor typhus. They will stand; they will dig their dugouts; they will sleep in the rain; they will stand until there is an order to go. The anticipation of Russia.... The thrill of expectation is in the breath of the white birds, in the rustle of the banner tassels hanging from the shafts. The anticipation of Russia is in the beckoning flight of the evening's dawn that the blue trumpeter sings to all four corners of the world. It is in every silent gaze. It is in dreams, in the inaudible prayers that only the white birds know about, that fall, having folded their wings, in light rows along the blue valley.

Turkul and Manstein see me off.... I understand now why their general's tent seemed to me a cold casemate, where the walls are scrawled with mute cries of monograms and curses, where proud and fearsome captive birds beat their wings impatiently. I understand now why there was gossip in the camps about the attempt of these generals to march on Constantinople. I also understand that one night in winter when the two of them rushed into the icy water to attack a French torpedo boat. They were sitting in a coffee shop by the breakwater. Suddenly they decided to seize a torpedo boat looming in the fog near the breakwater with its guard lights on. They grabbed their Nagants, both jumped in, and swam off.... They were taken aboard by a Russian barque, and they grumbled unhappily.

They walk beside me. I hear their stories from behind the glass, shaky wall, their short, calm words about the great bleeding. I shake Manstein's hand and, noticing the rim of a wedding ring on his dry finger, I ask, "Pardon me, are you married?"

"Yes. My wife is with me, but my little girl has died...."

The white birds froze in the valley. The blue night is descending from the mountains and is already spreading its delicate robes over the birds, studded with stardust.

I know that there are sentries at the straw tents, where the rolled-up banners are slumbering. The shreds of the age-old banner's brocade whisper to the stars about their wonderful native land.

And the sentries listen to the night, the stars and the whispers of the brocade.

We walk toward the city with the artillery lieutenant Misha, who is shy and quiet, like Second Lieutenant Romashov from Kuprin's *The Duel*. Misha dropped out of university and enlisted as a volunteer near Rostov. He knows many stories from behind the glass wall, many slow clenched words about the great bleeding. He has gulped every drop from the depths of the war—this russet-headed, big-eyed boy with sensitive, nervous nostrils. When he speaks, his face pales, and his nostrils dilate and flutter anxiously.

"I enlisted because I believed in our cause," says Misha. "And all the young people in the army are like me: believers. We went because our faith was our condemnation. And maybe we were all condemned to die for Russia.... Do you think in our hearts we didn't know that we were tragically outnumbered, that the Bolsheviks were being helped by historical luck, while we were doomed to die? Let history be ruthless, but it is just, and this is not about us, but about historical justice; this is about our faith that Russia is calm, and not rabid. That Russia will be built by peace, and not by war. We believed, we, the condemned—do you understand?"

"Yes."

"Well, then. We fought and we imagined that they were thinking about us. All we had to do was to win and they would build everything for us.... Only now we saw that there is emptiness all around us. We are alone. And beyond Gallipoli, beyond our monastery wall, there's emptiness and devastated souls. Do you understand me?"

"Yes, yes. Go on," I replied to his nervous, sorrowful question.

"They say over there that we are dead men. But we aren't dead men as long as that for which we went to die is still alive. We did not want generals or tsars; we are not the cannon fodder of generals' schemes, but we are the living fodder of Russia herself.... And we were torn out in blood. We could not resist. And here we are. Maybe we are dead men, if Russia herself is dead. Maybe we are not needed if Russia is not needed. But she is alive, and don't you realize that we, like her, are alive too?

"We had some sort of selection process in Gallipoli," Misha added after a moment's silence. "Those who couldn't stand the trials left. Those who didn't want our canned goods left, those who couldn't languish in inaction, those who were suffocating and couldn't overcome our iron discipline. There may still be some canned-food-whiners and some downtrodden, but the majority, I know it, are ready for new trials. We are all, here, test subjects for Russia. Here is the test, here, in Gallipoli; history sets its own test, whether there will be a Russia or not. We have been cleansed of all the festering pus of war; we have whitened ourselves. We have become the living idea of Russia, and if she is alive, we are not dead either, because we carry Russia in us like the sun. And that is why everyone here has a burning soul."

Misha cast his pale face up to the sky and twitched his sensitive nostrils raggedly.

"Our souls burn like these here stars."

I stay silent, but I understand. Misha is a convert. Lieutenant Misha has forever taken communion with the White Order of Russia; Lieutenant Misha lives to die for his Fair Lady.

We walk along a bluish moonlit road. Far away, in the moonlit gloom, jackals call out in a long, humid howl. The jackals come out of the bendy thickets at night and sit on their hind legs and howl around the white camps, their gray muzzles raised to the moon.

"Do you hear," Misha says. "The jackals are howling. They howl every night. And sometimes it seems that the whole world around us is like the night and it howls like a jackal.

"Here, in Gallipoli, we are examining ourselves to our very core." Misha leans toward me. "We are looking into every nook and cranny of our souls. After all, Gallipoli is firstly—how should I say—self-education itself, the hardening of will and spirit. Here we do everything in order to return to Russia strong, forged, iron men, pure in spirit; and our whole army, all of our patience, is the great Russian conditioning. . . .

"I don't know, of course," said Misha, lightly touching my sleeve. "After all, all of us in the army are so ordinary, bad and good, but ordinary and inconspicuous people. . . . But it sometimes feels that our army is the national will of Russia. You see, all the blows, all the tempests of death and destruction were thrown by the Bolsheviks against the will, against the strength and thought of the Russian people. They had to strangle the national will, to crush it, to trample it in the blood of our national emergency, to eradicate Russia upon its devastated place, to carry out their vivisection, of the commune and of the Internationale. . . ."

Misha's hand lightly shudders on my elbow. "They almost succeeded. On the surface, they have squashed the national will with bayonets. Kornilov has fallen, Denikin, Kolchak, Wrangel. True Russian democracy—among the Cossacks—was exterminated. . . . They succeeded, but also didn't succeed at all. The Russian Army in Gallipoli stands under Kornilov's banners.

"That's the army which the rebel Kornilov took command of. Don't forget, he led it against Russian lack of will, against the turmoil of words and the turmoil of souls, against rebellion. There are Russian rebels in favor of rebellion against Russia. And there are rebels not in favor of Russian rebellion over Russia. We're the rebels who are against rebellion. The whole history of our White struggle is a national rebellion and national uprising against the weak-willed, merciless, and despicable Russian rebellion. . . .

"We are the national will. That is why we are alive; that is why we are immortal. We are alone, we are few, but we hear from over there, from Russia, our living breath of many millions. Russia will remain; we know this, and if Russia remains, so will we, because we are its immortal will to life. We are immortal. . . ."

The lieutenant's upturned face shines with the bluish glow of the moon.

Misha, a lieutenant, a dear lieutenant, a colonel, a captain, a gunner, a private—it doesn't matter who, whose names I do not know. . . . But, Misha, dear Lieutenant, you were pinned with bayonets by the sailors behind the Narva outpost in St. Petersburg, when Kornilov's mutinous regiments were pouring out of the revolutionary capital.

Dear Lieutenants, Captains, non-commissioned officers without surnames, you, clenching your teeth, fell under machine-gun fire in Moscow. You were abandoned on rotten straw in a Cossack hut because you were in agony. You suffocated and burned on infirmary beds from typhus. Freezing, you were taken off your horse. At Manych and Orel, and at Kursk, you fell on the road, arms flung out convulsively, casting aside your blackened rifle, heated by gunfire and your green duffel bag. . . .

Dear Lieutenants, Captains, Corporals, Bombardiers, Gunners

without surnames—you were forgotten, abandoned in the shivering and animal turmoil of Novorossiysk and Odessa. You were infested with lice in the cold, swarming holds of transports. In Constantinople, beyond the barbed wire of the camps, you were shoved into the pit of a mass grave by the shoe of a blue French sergeant....

This dear lieutenant, a pale boy, with quietly blazing dark eyes, walks beside me, and his upturned, thin face glows in the moonlight.

Our road takes us past the Russian brotherly cemetery. High on the mountain slope, between the light shadows of the crosses, the heavy stone bell of the Russian tombstone to the memory of the Zaporozhians who died in Turkish captivity, to the memory of the prisoners of 1854, to the memory of the Russian soldiers of 1920–1921, is graying.

There is a bronze plaque on the tombstone, with the words of General Kutepov's decree: "Let everyone, from general to soldier, bring forth one stone for the construction of this monument...." And to this place, from the city and camps, for many days, came a quiet pilgrimage of Russian regiments, gray-haired generals, children, priests, soldiers, Sisters of Charity, Junkers, the sick from the infirmaries....

Wreaths of thorns made of rusty barbed wire, crossed cannons, and swords cut from tin. The brown mounds of the graves are blanketed with St. George's ribbons. Light iron crosses shine through the lunar gloom. Night walks among the graves, a silent night....

Here they are, nameless, brotherly.

Here are the graves of the children. Here is a tin plaque: "Bombardier of the artillery battery Simon Kruglov." Here

General Kutepov by the monument to the Russian soldiers of Gallipoli, 1921

inscriptions in ink pen: "To my dear brother," "Sleep peacefully, my friend." Here is the grave of the young poet Rutkovsky, a Junker who burned to death of fever in spring. The grave grasses, fresh from the breath of the night, are perhaps whispering in the unspoken, vague whispers of his young poems ... about the lights of hometowns, about the foggy and alien lights of hometowns, from which they leave on a night march, retreating; the gray tale of the autumn rain, when one dozes off in the saddle on long cavalry marches; of the morning singing of the silver signal trumpet, raised toward the dawn and the sun. . . .

The Russian white cemetery by the white ghostly Russian monastery. The cemetery of those who fell by the imperceptible walls of Jerusalem. And of those who shot themselves, burning in the fire of slow anticipation and longing, and of those who died silently in fevers, from hunger, under the fiery paw of typhus.

By the gray tombstone, the shadow of a sentry grows cold. Above his head, on the yellowish marble, a two-headed eagle spreads its formidable wings, sinks its knotty claws into the marble and tears at it, and the eagle's eyes are set in wrathful sorrow.

The sentry stares intently into the distance, through the lunar gloom, to where the white birds sleep, blanketed by the delicate cover of starry robes.

The Scatter of Stars

I sleep above a cliff, by the sea.

You wrap yourself in a blanket, lie down on the warmed ground, on the thorns of gray grass, and all night long the wind from the sea rustles soft gusts in your ears and sweeps across your face with a fresh tremor. At daybreak your shirt and blanket become damp with dew, and your face and hands smell of sea freshness.

Up over the cliff, soldiers and officers sleep intermingled. In the wooden houses the stifling night air is unbearable. They sleep, as I do, on the ground, wrapped in blankets, and only some of them make creaky and unstable beds out of planks from the crates for canned food, lest a centipede or a scorpion should strike them on the legs at a late hour of the night.

Along the cliff, in the clayey brown sand, dugouts have been dug up, into which they crawl on their knees. And below us, lower down, on the plateau, at night, sleeping people are spread out on the ground in the same way. A thin, silvery, and very shamefaced horn of the moon walks shyly over all of us at night, which soaks and drags its slender, bashful chain of light along the sea.

The lower plateau slopes off toward the sea. There's a gray road, gray fences made of good-sized stones, and further down, a house with a round gable whitens, where General Kutepov lives. And behind the house, foggy herds of the surf rumble.

"Greetings.... Greetings.... Sir!"

The clear early morning air is tearing and ringing with the cheerful greetings of Kutepov's convoys. The general gets up at first light.

There's stirring on our cliff too. Sleepy, they pull yellow soldier's pants over their underpants, sniffling. They sit down on the ground and wrap their legs in brown English wrappings, so long, a fathom long.

Long-haired, pale, thick-nosed Greek women with black manes of uncombed hair bang their shutters and stand in the squares of the windows in their shirts, shaking out their various home possessions onto the vegetable gardens.

Their possessions audibly clang in the morning silence.

The sun emerges from a blue flock of clouds, which have just taken a nap right up to the dawn. It was once just a scarlet crepuscular circle, but now it is like a round shield cast of clear yellow gold. The tender lump of a golden kitten climbs by a thread into the gentle blue of the sky.

And on the grass, clear and yellow as gold, there is a flutter of blue shadows. Clear gold on the soldiers' faces, drops of wet gold in their squinting, sleepy eyes. My neighbor, a tall, gaunt, one-year volunteer from the aviation detachment, holds his face up to the sky. The one-year volunteer is snub-nosed, and one of his eyes is brown, while the other is a pure blue. The different-eyed, one-year volunteer is an incorrigible merrymaker and joker.

"Hahahahaha," he greets the morning with a joyful bellowing.

And the golden kitten has already unleashed its claws, and the back of my neck is hot, and I have to get up; I have to shake out my possessions.

A dazzling golden tiger walks in the blue desert, launching millions of fiery claws into the earth.

In our gray house, down below, there's a commotion: morning tea is being brewed. The fire was built under the crumbling stone hearth, and they put their cans and tins on the fire one by one, queued, in a shaggy tuft of black soot and char.

They wear only pants, without shirts. Bronze backs and bronze faces are covered with soot. Their eyes are all smeared. They walk like devils at a furnace, conjuring over the bubbling, boiling water, squatting together, soldiers and officers alike.

They gently give way to each other. Gently, so as not to be noticed, they try to do each other a thousand little favors, a thousand little, small human pleasantries.

"Mr. Lieutenant, I'll lend you some brushwood."

"It's fine, it's fine, thank you. . . . Lend me some please."

"You'd better toss in the tea, Sapunov; it's boiling."

"Right away, Mr. Rottmeister; I just need to dart upstairs."

"Why go upstairs? Just take a pinch from me."

Here everyone speaks formally; there is a soft caution and a soft politeness in every gesture.

The hearth is smoking. The smoke stabs at their eyes, and everyone rubs them, squinting and puffing, like young devil-puppies beside a furnace.

The clawing sun had already heated the dust hanging over the white landing. By the cargo trucks, morning classes had begun.

They're being taught about the engine. A bunch of white shirts are standing in the wasteland by the trucks, and one of them explains in a bass voice, with a velvety croak.

"If, now, the cylinder is tilted, that's when the explosion occurs.... Is that clear?"

"That's right. If the cylinder is tilted...."

Balancing and wobbling along the road near the stone-gray ridge of the Turkish cemetery, soldiers with homemade buckets over their shoulders are advancing along the road in a single file. These are the day watchmen fetching fresh water from the fountains.

Water jingles joyfully in the tin containers. It splashes, and wet dark blotches of splashed water stretch behind the watchmen on the gray dust.

My neighbor, the one-year volunteer, was also walking along with the buckets. He saw me, squinted first his brown and then his blue eye, and smiled.

"Watch out.... The water-bearers are marching."

Behind the stone ridge, on the wastelands, where rows of heavy slabs are stacked like a row of cyclopes, white flocks of white shirts sit. They scowl gloomily in the sunlight, rustle their notebooks, and write; and the little officer-professor's huge spectacles glare at the sky with sheaves of dazzling rays.

"Now we will draw the parabola toward point B...."

On a rusty iron board there are segments and sectors drawn in chalk, descending arches of lines, and a white jumble of algebraic formulas.

A Turkish girl and a Turkish boy in a red fez, burning in the sun like a ruby, clung to the crevices in the stone ridge. They both stretched out their thin golden faces and stared with all their brown eyes at the sheaves of dazzling rays from the *effendi's* fearsome spectacles.[16] They stared and whispered in fear.

In front of the shop of the Zemstvo-City Union, military wives stand in a line. Many have children in their arms. They are waiting in line for some of the zemstvo's bread and porridge.

To the beach, with caps pulled down to their foreheads, swimmers streamed in. A White Guard strode by with boots crunching hard and evenly. Everyone waves him away with their hands at once. They wave him away and chant a robust chorus:

"Hey, ho, no worry over woe...."

And the clawed sun is already casting a golden haze of heat. The dampness presses down by midday like a millstone. At midday, white dust sleepily wanders across the charred wastelands.

The Earrings, glossy with sweat, are half asleep on the clock, and wobble with their black, skinny legs spread out in a circular pattern. Some of the stalls are closed up with shutters. Rough, shaggy dogs climb into the marble basins of the exhausted fountains, seeking coolness and shade on the chilly stone.

In the coffee houses at noon they sip bitter coffee from white cups, drinking each hot sip with cold, clear water from fogged, tinkling glasses. In the stalls, at the counters, Russian soldiers are selling plump-cheeked tomatoes, for a long time, without hurry, and sharing melon among themselves, cutting it into moist, orange slices. On the counter there are mounds of green crusts and a wet mess of fibrous melon seeds.

A dusty emptiness.

The sea falls silent in the golden gloom of the heat. The sea becomes muffled and covered with a lilac mist.

---

[16] Title of nobility in Turkish; can also mean "sir."

And until the evening there are heat and white, dusty emptiness.

Until evening, when the sun turns yellow and cools down and the blue clouds begin to look for an easy night's lodging near it. Until evening, when the glittering spears of the sun will rise above the blue line of the mountains and become motionless. And the raised spears of the solar guards will freeze and will then be extinguished in the evening ocean. And then the scarlet ocean will recede and drift away behind the mountains without a sound.

And a blue and gentle evening will then sound over Gallipoli.

A cornet somewhere sings with a lonely sound, cooing. Somewhere two female voices sounded: slender and affectionate. They sing from "The Queen of Spades."

"It's evening, the clouds have faded. . . ."

Likely, students of an art studio are learning a duet for an evening concert.

Inside the cargo truck, near which in the morning someone had taught a bunch of white shirts about explosions in a tilted cylinder, two soldiers now sit in the worn leather seat. They put their feet on the round steering wheel and bent forward with their chins. One has a book open in his lap. Both lean over the white pages, and I can hear how one of them says, *"Der Garten ist grün. Der Garten ist grün. . . ."*

And the other turns away from his neighbor and repeats, like a tongue twister, *"Ich bin, du bist, er, sie ist. . . ."*

They're learning a foreign language. People study here at foreign language courses, at the national university, in schools, in the gymnasium, in the library. They study by rewriting textbooks, one notebook at a time. They study voraciously. There has already been a graduation of young officers; senior classes are being examined in the gymnasium; thousands have attended the national university, and hundreds of them are now speaking French and English in the camps with desperate Russian "ehs" and "umms," but already very confidently and lively.

There are up to six thousand Russian students in Gallipoli. In Gallipoli there are up to twenty thousand young peasant boys, yesterday's Russian factory boys, yesterday's gymnasium students and office workers.

The Russian youth is carrying out a monastic feat in Gallipoli. Where is there still such a Russian youth, so radiant in spirit, who condemned themselves to blood and feat, who went into the white monastery of Gallipoli for a locked-up, untainted novitiate? Our green garden, our dear Russian hope, the Russian youth, our novice Alyosha,[17] the third of the brothers, the youngest, one who will replace us all—he will replace the cold Russian madmen-Ivans, who are kindred to the devil, and the Don Quixotes-Mityas, who have wasted their souls, and the vile Smerdyakovs. The third brother, dear Alyosha, behind whom, swathed in great blood and festering pus, is the third Russia.

The blue evening was already here. The opened book is barely visible, but they continue repeating German words in the truck. Enough is enough, gentlemen; listen how the evening resounds and the stars, high and misty, appear in timid, shimmering crowds. . . . Enough, gentlemen!

"Der Garten ist grün. Der Garten ist grün. . . ." continues reaching me as I walk away.

I love to walk the streets as they turn blue in the evening.

Cigarettes burn their red dots along my way. Voices sound with

---

[17] Referring to the three famous Russian bogatyrs: Ilya Muromets, Dobrynya Nikitich, and Alyosha Popovich.

a hushed murmur. The ruins of the walls shine quietly—blue, listening.

The blue evening listens, and everyone hears its delicate and cautious breathing. The dust, falling asleep, and the marble turbans in the weeds, and the gray Greek houses, and the people, creaking like decrepit old men, can also hear it.

The music of the blue evening is skittish and flies off from the loud chatter, from the stomping, from the jolting rattle of carts. The music of the evening is skittish, and that is why voices sound so cautiously and so delicately, and people pass by so quietly, without stomping, and that is why the cigarette lights smolder so softly.

On the stone steps near the gray houses and on the slopes near the Turkish cemetery, soldiers sit in slightly whitened flocks. They are listening to the evening, and their evening chatter is soft and quiet. Someone laughs, but the laughter is muted. Their laughter is like a quiet splash in a dark pond, when the water spreads in silvery circles from a silver roach playing.

Everything is ghostly, and everything is gentle in the blue air. I listen to fragments of soft Russian speech, and they form a kind of evening song. I walk and want to figure out, want to pick out all the trembling chords of this song, but I can't, and it pains me that I can't.

"Tomorrow we have to go together," comes from the blue gloom.

"And she was all snow-white, and she said *merci* in French, and everything was as it should be. I met her in Odessa. Well, all right. . . ."

"The Reds hacked him to death with their sabers. The Budyonovtsy rode in. They were crushing us like hell. And he was left beneath the horses."

"I'm lying down, on the lookout, and she's coming at me, and she's turning across the field toward me. Old woman. I can tell from the moonlight. 'Soldier,' she says, 'don't shoot; give me a drink.' I give her a drink, and scold her: 'How did you get here?' 'From across the Dnieper, through the swamps. To my son. My son is serving in your Whites.' Then I said to her, 'Go, woman, go to the division headquarters....'"

"We were standing near Kakhovka. We were harassing the infantry...."

"And I'll tell you what: they say all the states will march to Russia in order to restore order...."

"You say oats. Your oats may be good, but you've seen what kind of wheat we have in Melitopol...."

I listen to the evening chatter of the soldiers, and it occurs to me that in the same way, in the blue evening, Skobelev's soldiers spoke in a soft chatter about camps, division headquarters, and campaigns in their camps near Tashkent, and Empress Elisabeth's powdered guards at their tents near Berlin, and Alexander I's mustached carabineers around bonfires on the sidewalks of Parisian suburbs....

I head to the sea, to the rocks. The rough stone is already cool. Above me, on the slope, four shirts appear slightly white. No faces are visible in the blue twilight. The lonely flame of a cigarette smolders. I listen.

"You were a gunner—how would you know anything about the shaft horses? Meanwhile, I've been driving our troika for four years. I know them both, the horses. The left redhead, young, called Leda, and the right one was also redheaded, but with a gnarled face, big-bottomed, and she had a granny owner who was run over, and she squatted on her hind legs, and her name was Dreamy. I'll tell you all about them. There was no better than my red-haired Leda when it came to carrying cargo. She carried equipment with a forward spirit, her chest like the wind, and Dreamy, of course, is a diligent mare, but how can she keep up with Leda, when she pulls with her back, and not with her chest.... Do you remember how our battery was downed near Novorossiysk? Dreamy was hit in the belly by a shell; her intestines spilled out. We were moving out, and she, my brother, she jerked her head and started to get up. And she did get up. And followed us, her guts dragging under her belly. She soon got left behind.... And yet, Leda reached Novorossiysk. There we abandoned her while preparing for our next march. The horses were walking on the ice near the breakwater, thirsty, unfed. They walked in herds and kept coming closer to the water. The water smelled of dampness, but all they wanted to do was drink, the horses. So, the herd comes up to the breakwater, and we were already sitting on the ships. I have an eye for horses. I see my redhead in the herd. She pulls her head to the water, roars, and her nostrils flutter. She's thirsty. 'Agh,' I think, 'Leda.' And I see, my brother, all of a sudden Leda leaps from all four legs and into the water. She couldn't stand the thirst.... She collapsed, touched the salt of the sea with her lips and pulled her head back. She pulled her head back, and the water started carrying her off, that Leda. I walked away, brother; I didn't look, but of course she drowned...."

They went silent on the slope. And the misty scatter of stars listened to the human silence....

"Yes, this here is Russia...." General Kartsev, gently rolling his cloudy, gray eyes at me, spoke to me in the cafe where I had come from the sea to drink a glass of wine.

General Kartsev is the chairman of the court of honor. General Kartsev is an old military pedagogue, a theoretician of war, a connoisseur of the Russian army, a traveler, and a warrior.

General Kartsev is a soldier by blood; even his great-grand-fathers served in the Leib Guard. There seems to have been no war, no Russian campaign since the eighties, where General Kartsev had not taken part. On his worn jacket there was only one decoration: a steel sword with a steel wreath of thorns on a St. George's ribbon, the symbol of the Kornilov Ice March. And from the silver embossing of his Cossack saber dangles a worn, twisted scrap of the St. George's ribbon, which is bestowed on the brave.

General Kartsev is heavyset and bald. He is chubby, his eyes bulge outwards, and his gray beard snakes out of his neck. General Kartsev—the president of the court of honor, the god of war, as the young officers in Gallipoli call him—looks like Socrates.

He has recently lost his last dear person in this world. His bulging eyes are always moist, and, to tell the truth, he does not refuse an extra glass of tart red wine or cinnamon-scented brown brandy anymore.

His conversational style is wise and beautiful. His aged, bulging eyes have seen many things: India, the steppes of Tibet, Paris, Japan, campaigns and quiet books, the lights of bivouacs and the green lamps of libraries. His valuable archives, the correspondence of his fathers and grandfathers with the tsars and his diaries, all perished.

I tell him about what I saw in Gallipoli, about the soldiers, about Lieutenant Misha, about the saltpeter sores, about the one-year volunteer with brown and blue eyes. I tell him that I have heard the living heart of Russia beating here, under the folded-up banners.

"Russia breathes here," Kartsev said. "I don't know how it is with you emigrants, but here Russia is alive. Russia is beautiful, pure, chivalrous. I'm going to Constantinople. You know, a Russian officer challenged the French lieutenant Boucher to a duel. Boucher was rude to a Russian woman, the wife of a Russian officer. A challenge was sent. Bouchet replied with some vague letter, either a refusal, or an apology, and then a French representative replied something like this: that since we eat their canned food, what honor could we ever possess. We replied that a soldier's honor and canned food are different things. We said that we would inform the neighboring armies how the French officer refused to step up to the challenge. And now I'm being summoned by the Commander of the French Corps to Constantinople."

The god of war grins, casting his slightly glittering eyes at me.

"And that Russia is alive here: that's exactly right. Listen to the army and you will hear that Russia is alive. You see, my dear fellow, you thought of the former Army from Kuprin's *The Duel*, from the Romashovs, Captains Sliva and Shurochka in stockings with arrows, but you knew nothing about our Army, about Gallipoli. You see, if you over there fail to hear what is going on here, an irreparable mistake will be made there. These aren't the regurgitated remains from the Civil War, or some black rabble, or plunderers. This is the new army, the pure cadre of Russia, which has passed through all the trials, beyond imagination."

The general drinks wine in slow sips, wets his mustache, and drops of wine hang like rubies on the gray ends of his whiskers.

"We understand things here in a different way than in the newspapers. Don't the Reds have an army? And a very strong army at that. The Reds have good, talented commanders. There are many scoundrels in the world, but we will never sit with scoundrels at the same table, even if they chop off my head, at the neck.... We are not politicians, but we have our own soldiers' religion: Satan and God fight in the world. Today Satan won. But we will win, because God is with us. That's what we believe. And that is why we endure every trial and display great human patience."

The old man lowered his weighty head on his hand. He brooded beside the table, like an old knight from a long-read fairy tale, like a gray-haired and weighty master of a knightly Order.

"Try to understand the army.... You must have laughed, like everybody else, at such stupidity. Do you know that the strongest armies are those where each regiment, each unit is different, blooms in its own way, carefully preserves its historical memories, its covenants of blood and exploits. The German army is an example. The death of an army is in its leveling, in the numbering of regiments, in gray ranks, when all colors fade, when the blooming soul of the army withers away. And you will remember how the French 'numbered' army fled from Charleroi under the blows of, I think, Pomeranian grenadiers. Our army blossomed under Elizabeth and Suvorov. Our army began to wither away from Milyutin's leveling, from Vannovsky's numbered regiments. There came the officers, the numbers, the millions of bearded masses, total gray pawns.... The army was sustained by people you've never seen. The army was held by hermit officers, monk officers, who knew nothing but their regiments and soldiers. They came here too, men for whom the regiment, the company, the platoon, was dearer than anything else in the world, dearer than a beloved."

As I listen to the general's paradoxes, a humorous fragment

from the *Zhuravl (Crane)* comes to my mind and I begin to understand its meaning in a new way. . . .

"He who's colored like a poster

"He must be Kornilov's soldier. . . ."

Perhaps that is the way it should be, to be painted, to bloom with one's own color, to sing with one's own tone. The young regiments in Gallipoli jealously guard all their new insignia from the Civil War: patches on their sleeves, skulls on crossed swords, the black and red epaulettes of the Kornilovtsy, the crimson velvet of the epaulettes of the Drozdovtsy, and in the Old Guard the yellow shoulder cord of the axelbants, with a silver monogram of Catherine II, is carefully handed down in accordance with seniority. . . .

It's nighttime outside. . . .

A starry scattering of luminous fog shimmers over Gallipoli. A lighthouse beam flies through the starry fog in a golden shadow, falling on the dark sea with golden fluttering wings. Far away is the white tower of a lighthouse, the Fener, as the Turks call it. Yesterday I was there with some friends. . . . I did not expect to meet the artist Astrova here, the light, joyful comedy artist of our South. She followed her husband, an artillery captain, to Gallipoli. Plenitskaya and the young Kovalevskaya from the Alexandria stage are here as well.

I walk down a late-night street and remember how Astrova looked at me with both amusement and glee.

"So, you're leaving us? That's a shame, a shame. . . . I feel sorry for you, that you're leaving. . . . Russia isn't to be found anywhere in your Parises and Constantinoples. But here: we've got Russia. I feel sorry for you, that you're leaving."

I walk under a starry shimmer. The sighs of copper trumpets, far away, sing an old waltz. In the black water near the break-water, the blue lights of the stars sway like bashful fireflies, and the reflections of the cafe windows swell. The reflections are like long and delicate eyelashes.

On the float, at a narrow table, I meet Lukoshkov, commander of the Guards infantry. By the dark railing of the veranda, the water breathes a cold freshness of the night. The bright, sensitive, and nearby stars stand in a quiet crowd.

A light felucca sleeps, hoisting its slanting mast, and in the black cobweb of its gear the scatter of stars faintly trembles. The felucca may not be sleeping, but daydreaming and listening.

Guardsman Lukoshkov is slender and pale. On his white shoulder the yellow cord of an axelbant with Catherine's mono-gram tinkles slightly with its ends. Lukoshkov is a St. Petersburg Guardsman, polished to the nails, gentle, affable, but so reserved. And now the stars have come close to us, and I see in his eyes a quiet, and blue, glimmer of stars. And maybe that is why our glimmering conversation is so strange.

"The world has lost its beauty," Lukoshkov says, stroking his chin with his long fingers. "Beauty has withdrawn from the world. Everyone lives by the flesh. The soul of the world is being dragged through the mud. The world has no inspiration. The world of today has no wings, after the war."

Clinking his ring on the glass, he pours himself a glass of wine. He looks out at the scatter of stars, and he tells me a strange story, of a strange, chivalric love. . . . His friend has lost his beloved. His friend is alone under the stars, and his beloved has died. And there is nothing to forget by, and it can never be forgotten. But his Beloved will return, because Love is immortal, Love is undying, and its white color never withers. His Beloved will return, as a star falls to the earth, and his friend will meet her, perhaps here on earth, or perhaps wherever the starry mists shine.

I walk alone in the mist of stars. I walk to my cliff edge and think that such stories have already been forgotten among us. Such chivalrous stories of Undying Love and of the Fair Lady.

When I pass by the curtained window of the landing where you live, my dear, you will already be asleep. Just as you slept as a child, long ago, in St. Petersburg, with your scarlet-burning cheek pressed against your bent, white hand. And your chestnut braid will go loose and lightly tickle your sensitive eyelashes.

You'll be asleep by then, my darling. And if you weren't asleep, I would squat down on the floor by your mattress and tell you wonderful and strange stories about explosions in tilted cylinders, about trajectories and parabolas in wastelands, about German vocalizations in cars, about Leda the red-haired mare, about knights and chivalrous love.

Do you remember how long ago, when we were kids, our brother Zhenya used to assure us that at night, in the kitchen, he would sit on a stool, take a big teapot for the road, so that there would be something to drink on the way, and fly away on the stool to travel through the starry sky?

Do you remember when he told us of how the stars met him, where angels live? There are mournful angels, and their wings, dark as sorrow, are folded, and they look down on the earth sorrowfully at night. There are merry angels. They sing in the evening, and their singing makes the earth resound.... Do you remember when Zhenya assured us that the angels practice on their pianos, like you, and that they have, like our grandmother, cages with grumpy old parrots?

Are you sleeping? I've come to tell you strange tales of stars scattered on the earth, tales of people whose souls burn like stars.

Clouds

The ebb....

Gray herds of foam had smoothed the sand with yellowish, damp mirrors and left far into the sea. A specular road has stretched out on the sand all along the shore.

I stand by the shore and see in the damp mirrors at my feet the reflections of white clouds slowly moving in the sky.

Pierced by light, they billow golden smoke. Soon the sun will be setting, and the sky has brightened, turning blue, pure and quiet, before the evening comes.

In the damp mirrors the clouds billow slow clusters of pearls. Fluffy caps of snowy mountains are passing by. Caravans of white camels move, flashing blue between their white humps. Silent towers drift by. White knights' bands march with their shields raised.

The clouds leave—and are found again....

Maybe I can see on the damp sand the knightly shadows of the crusaders that pass through the high evening sky over Gallipoli, looking for the campsites of the knights' tents, looking for the stalls where the heavy horses neigh and the altars where the priors pray.

The knights are clouds; the clouds are knights....

White knights now exist only in children's fairy tales. There are no more knights in the world. The honorable world now wears a round, yellow canotier and picks at its golden fillings with a toothpick. The honorable world, smoking with sweat on the back of its neck, shakes the fiery floors of cafes with the horse stomp of the foxtrot.

The old pipers still sing of the priestly Christ, still dig through the worm-eaten Shakespeare, still lull at the pages of Goethe. The old pipers crank the lever of a hoarse barrel organ and drag out a rusted tune that there is a God, truth, and beauty, that mankind is the Son of God, bearing the radiance of divine light, the stellar cross.

The roar of the Canet and Bertha cannons and the weighty cylinder of the 14-inch guns from the dreadnaught are much more convincing than the old pipers. There's blood, and there's might, and there's no need to drag out the rusted tune any longer.

"Hey, gallop into a two-step; hey, kick your frenzied heels into a foxtrot."

For far too long Mr. Canet and Mr. Krupp have been talking. The world may be deaf and blind, but the world has decided that everything is permissible, because might and blood allow everything. And that is why, with their shaved necks crimson with blood, tucked into the tight collars of their uniforms, the German generals sat down at the Brest-Lithuanian table. And so, between golf and roast beef, the cheerful Lloyd George signed the British charter to buy the Russian carrion. And so in 1921 Anno Domini, the Parisian newspaper *Paris-Midi*, after reporting on Russia's starving to death, respectfully advising to help, respectfully advises the whole world not to forget that the life of one French-man is worth the life of ten thousand Russians.

"Hey, gallop into a two-step; hey, kick your frenzied heels into a foxtrot."

Satan now cranks the lever of the barrel organ. And this is more cheerful than the howling of old beggars on the cathedral porches, where the gray stone rumbles under the archways with the age-old whispers of unrequited prayers and unfulfilled hopes for a phantasmal Messiah.

The real Messiah has already arrived. Here he is, in a yellow canotier with gold fillings on his rotten teeth and an issue of *Paris-Midi* in the pocket of his ironed jacket.

Is it for him that the pilgrims went to Jerusalem, and Giordano Bruno went to the stake, and Camille Desmoulins sang the merc-ies of freedom, and the little drummer led the old guard into the fire? Or are these only clouds, clouds that pass high above the earth?

The Messiah, with his canotier in his hand, cranks the lever of the screeching barrel organ. Everything is permitted, and there will be no more light, and the sky is covered with blood.

The light has faded, and the sky is covered in blood, because my native land has faded.

My native land has turned to black, and the flame is already on the verge of burning up.

My native land, my icy desert. My native land, the devoured carrion that is showing its charred black ribs to the smoky, red sky.

Flakes of ashes have risen from my land, and the afterglow of my land is marching through fields of men.

My native land, you are the stench of cemeteries, and you are the night, and your dead move like wind all over the world. They tug on the rough ropes of the church bells. They breathe frost under the powdered, heavy wigs of legislators. They sit at the same table with those who trade in the dust of your cemeteries, my native land.

You are the night, my land, and night is upon the entire world. You are a cemetery, and the dying spirit of the cemetery is upon the entire world. A beast howls in your icy deserts, my land, and throughout the whole world the beast howls, grinning its daggers of golden fillings at the terror of fatal longing.

Night has fallen. The expected time of the Apocalypse, when the third angel poured out his cup and great blood was shed, is oozing, slowly.... But there will be day. You, my land, are as the dawning of a new kingdom, and you shall be the day, my land. You, my land, will be like a wife, clothed with the sun.

Clouds.... White smoke in damp mirrors. White towers float silently by.

High above the blue sea the monastery towers gleam white. It is quiet in the monastery, and the sea barely carries the rumble of the earth to it. Warrior-monks live there. They came from a world of blood. They took their youth and their children behind the white walls. They've brought faith and beauty there.

They've brought a stellar cross with them into the white monastery. They've closed themselves in. They are like the last glimmer of light in a black sky, the last glimmer that promises the wished-for dawn.

The radiant army, the white phantom, is already blessedly streaming over Russia. Imperishable white roses are growing on the black Russian cross....

The stellar cross burns high in the night sky.

There will be a silent dawn. And in the dawn the phantom knights will come, white warrior-monks. They will bring divine light and hidden stars to the world.

They were born in blood, the white warriors. They are the spawn of war. They are the children of suffering and abuse. But the weight of war has been washed away in a monastery over the blue sea, and there the war has revealed its other face, bright and benevolent....

It's time for me to go to the steamer. Already my blue-tinged shadow on the yellow sand is getting longer, in accord with the evening. The turf rustles sleepily under my steps.... I recall the white camps, the rustling of straw against the tents where the banners lie, the White soldiers, the Socrates-like Kartsev, the one-year volunteer with brown and blue eyes, and the artillery lieutenant Misha.

Why do they all look the same to me, and why does a single flame burn in their tired eyes? The joyful flame of a conquering spirit.

In the white monastery, a gentle and pure master-monk, as gentle and pure as the angelic Fra Angelico, outlined the first contours of a divine fresco. Still vague, barely perceptible, marvelous and beautiful outlines of Russia....

The gray-haired Kartsev, whose great-grandfathers had served as companions and sergeants in the Imperial Guard; and the differently-eyed one-year volunteer of the Popoviches, whose grandfathers may have sung memorial services in trembling voices for the Boyars killed at Borodino and on the Smolensk road; the corporals from the Voronezh Red Army; the colonels of the St. Petersburg Guards—all are illuminated by the quiet dawn of Russia.

Russia breathes in Gallipoli. Moscow's courtyards, overgrown with soft grass and drowned in the sun, breathe here. Here floats the quiet fire of the evening dawn in the windows of palaces on the English Embankment of St. Petersburg, when the Admiralty's steeple is extinguished in the pale sky by a yellow arrow. Here the honeyed smell of Russian buckwheat is fresh, when the rain sweeps its nets joyfully across the streaming, blue sky over the roaring Russian stretches and forests. Russia shines and gleams here.

Gallipoli is the sludge of Russia, a Russia that knows no respite on its marvelous and terrible road.

If in 1854, near Sevastopol, the Russian army would have been thrown into the Black Sea, the artillery lieutenant Leo Tolstoy would have come here, to the Turkish camps.

The small, pale, and black-eyed Hussar Cornet Lermontov would have been on guard here, at the straw tents where the battle banners rest, leaning.

Pushkin, twirling and twisting loops of his reddish curls in his quick fingers, would sing lightly and inspirationally his "Epistles for Gallipolian Friends" about the joy of the triumphant spirit, about the day that will shine in the morning. . . .

Clouds, clouds. . . . My thoughts, too, are like clouds.

My shadow, breaking on the gray ridge of fences, runs up through the weeds. There's the plaza with the trucks and the gray house, where, at the top, under the tiled roof, is the blanket-covered window of your landing.

We walk together to the steamer. We don't talk about the long distances. We recall our home, our huge, black grand piano in the living room, and our old nanny Stepanida, whose teeth whistled as she spoke.

And while we reminisce, she laughs, and I see the wind lightly ruffling her chestnut curls on her white nape, permeated by the warm gilding of the sunset. I squeeze her dear hands tightly. I want to tell her that she is Russian, that I am proud of her, the wife of a Gallipoli officer, but I see her brown eyes pierced with evening gilding and I remember St. Petersburg, the frosty smoke of January, our brother Zhenya, and her green briefcase with a silver lock and key.

"So, what do you think, will we ever find your silver key?"

"We will. Of course. And then we'll open everything," she jokes quietly.

We are standing by the breakwater. Lightly splashing and rolling golden snakes from the oars, a sloop will soon approach from the steamer.

Sunset's hour. The sparkles of the raised spears of the sun cool over the blue ghosts of the mountains. An evening silence has approached the white birds.

The trumpeter sings the evening's dawn. I know that the scarlet sunset blazes on his copper. The trumpeter sings, raising his trumpet to the four corners of the world. The evening's dawn flies in with short cries, like a bird beating its scarlet wings.

Who are you calling, evening trumpeter?

In the cold of autumn, when the white birds will fly away, piles of burnt bricks from dismantled hearths will turn black on the brown and wet grass, rusty piles of tin cans will smoke in the rain, and the rain will wash away the clay steps of the Russian amphitheaters. And for a long time the autumn wind will carry white shreds of torn leaves.

When the white birds fly away, their bird tracks will remain in the valley: black, straight threads of ditches and paths, threaded like the loops of bird claws.

On the stony hills the rains will soak the two-headed eagles made of gray sea pebbles and shells. And the shells will resound with the melancholy sound of the tide.

On the brick walls of the houses and mosques of Gallipoli, when the white birds fly away, black eagles and black Russian letters will long darken: "Telegraph Company," "Artillery School," "Garrison Theater." And brown, little Turkish girls, listening to the howling of the damp wind and the rumbling of the tide, will sing the long songs of the Russian giaours.

When the white birds fly away, who will stand on an honored guard at the stone tombstone, where an eagle spreads its formidable wings, eyes set in wrathful sorrow?

The sun, releasing the last flocks of its scarlet birds from behind the blue mountains, will search the smoky valley for the trumpeter, when the white birds fly away.

"Where are you, my blue trumpeter?"

And above the smoky gloom of the sea, at dawn, there will be great luminous clouds. Towers, snowy mountains, caravans, and knights.

Clouds, clouds, clouds....

*   *   *

When the coals die out, touch them with your tongs, strike the charred black embers, and the sparks will rush and dance—sit closer, lean into the heat, and listen to the whispers of the fire.

Sit closer, bend forward, so that the crimson light illuminates your face, and listen to the whispers of the fire.

ENJOYED THIS BOOK?

TO READ MORE, VISIT US AT

ANTELOPEHILLPUBLISHING.COM